The Crisis of the
Middle Class

Henry Grayson

Associate Professor of Economics
University of Maryland

WITH A FOREWORD BY

Allan G. Gruchy

Professor of Economics
University of Maryland

Rinehart & Company, Inc.
New York

Not houses finely roofed or the stones of walls well-builded, nay nor canals and dockyards, make the city, but men able to use their opportunity.

ARISTIDES: Rhodian Oration

In memory of my uncle,

CHARLES JAMES GRAYSON

Foreword

Among the many great social changes now taking place there are none more important than the developments affecting the welfare and future prospects of the middle class. In the fluid Western society of the nineteenth century this vigorous class played a highly significant role as an agent of social and economic progress. Changes since the beginning of the present century, however, have threatened to weaken, if not to destroy, the function of the middle class as a dynamic source of further cultural advancement. A basic question now is, What is the future of the middle class in our large-scale society where huge aggregations of economic and political power such as the large corporation and the industrial union leave little scope for the free movement of the unorganized middle class? Is this class to be reduced to cultural impotence by the titanic struggles of entrenched economic and political privilege? Is the dynamic progressivism of the past century to which the middle class contributed so much to be followed by a stultifying staticism in the current century? In providing answers to these large and challenging questions Professor Grayson has developed an arresting theory of the middle class which merits the close attention of all those who are interested in the continued progress of Western civilization.

His analysis of the origins, development, and future of the

middle class is of both theoretical and pragmatic significance. As a study in social theory the analysis demonstrates in a new field the basic interrelations of the various social sciences. It is an excellent antidote to those unfortunate tendencies, now much too prominent in the work of social scientists, to pursue each social science as an all-absorbing specialty. In addition, his theory of the middle class reveals that methodology in the social sciences involves much more than a narrow search for only measurable variables. The study is a challenge to all social scientists who would reduce their science to mathematico-logical generalizations which, while quite useful in their proper place, are all too frequently taken to be the terminus rather than the halfway station in a broad understanding of human culture.

The pragmatic import of this analysis of the role of the middle class derives from Professor Grayson's cogent observation that the crisis of the middle class is in a larger sense the crisis of modern civilization. There is a need, as he points out, to cope with the existing cultural imbalance which finds its origins in the lag of social science behind natural science, and in the tendency for local loyalties to take precedence over broader and more abstract loyalties. If these cultural lags continue, there is a genuine danger that the middle class may lose its historic role as a cultural innovator. Although the theory of the middle class rises above mere ideological considerations, Professor Grayson does not fail to draw attention to the need for positive action if the cultural milieu in which this class thrives is to be preserved. While he is primarily interested in the analytical aspects of the problem of the middle class, his approach to this problem is functional. There is in this study of the middle class a highly successful blending of theory, methodology, and policy implications which, although they may not command the full assent of all social scientists, will nevertheless bring them face to face with a crucial issue of the twentieth century.

Allan G. Gruchy

Preface

———————◆———————

The middle class, as defined in this study, differs so radically from the meaning ordinarily connected with the term that some explanation of the vital differences is necessary. A member of the middle class, as understood in this study, is an individualist who may be anywhere in the social scale from the bottom to the top. The fundamental characteristic which marks him out as a member of the middle class is not his position in the social hierarchy, but rather his attitude toward the society in which he lives. If he is determined to move into a preferred position in the social scale, he is middle class. He is an energizer, a changer, a rearranger, whose fundamental purpose is not to tear down the society but to alter the structure in such a manner that he is an individual will attain a preferred position. When he ceases to seek a higher standing and concentrates upon maintaining the position he now has, then he is no longer a member of the middle class. He has become more interested in privilege and restriction than in change.

It should be pointed out that a middle class individualist may be highly conservative in some aspects of social life at the same time that he is insidiously bringing about change in other areas of social activity. Rarely is a middle class individualist an energizer in all aspects of his social life. Thus, the financial tycoon may be and often is a conservative in politics, a faithful member of an orthodox church, distrustful of innovation in education or in the arts.

This definition has been placed in the preface to provide the reader with a fair understanding concerning the nature of the theory. Such an appreciation will undoubtedly enrich his appraisal of the introductory chapters.

In this work I have deliberately attempted a fresh point of view. This does not mean that I am not deeply indebted to previous writers for many of the concepts. The influence of such writers as Pareto, Max Weber, Tawney, Toynbee, Mosca, Plato, to mention only a few, will be most apparent to the reader. Yet sometimes I did not obtain information from the source one might expect. As an example, it was my misfortune to work out the crisis theory of change quite independently during my student days, before I had heard of Toynbee (although I had read Herbert Spencer). It was a disillusioning experience to discover that the concept was already well established—and certainly an object lesson that reflection without extensive reading may be quite as fruitless as reading without independent reflection. All of the writers listed in the bibliography, as well as many others, have cast their shadow over the work. Any claim to originality must be in the synthesis of the concepts and in the manner in which they have been emphasized.

I am grateful to my colleagues at the University of Maryland for stimulating conversations concerning the study, and especially to Professors Eli W. Clemens, Dudley Dillard, Allan G. Gruchy, F. R. Root, Messrs. Walter Measday and E. A. Robinson, each of whom has read portions of the manuscript and has contributed comments and suggestions. I should also like to thank Professor Howard R. Bowen of Williams College for his encouraging comments on the finished work. I have adopted many of his suggestions, and hope he will be forbearing concerning those I have passed over. It would be unfair not to include among the acknowledgments the several hundred students who have endured my lectures in the subject. Their lively interest in the work and active participation in the discussions have been profoundly gratifying and encouraging. In addition, as always, I am deeply grateful to my wife for her courageous support and secretarial assistance. More than one idea was worked out in conversation over the dinner table, and it is probable that some of the interpretations emanated from her mind rather than from mine. Finally, I should like to thank the editors of Rinehart & Company for the meticulous care with which they have handled the problems of publication.

I am, of course, completely and solely responsible for all statements in this study.

Henry Grayson

University of Maryland
January 7, 1955

Contents

The Crisis of the Middle Class

CHAPTER ONE

The Eclectic Causal Theory

The Cycle of Civilizations

In order to appreciate the non-rational aspects of early social organization it is desirable to consider the group ethics of primitive man. Sir Arthur Keith and others have advanced the theory that primitive man was not a solitary creature engaged with all outside forces in a lonely struggle for survival.[1] According to Keith's argument, primitive man was from the outset of the species a social creature congregated into small groups of forty to eighty members. V. Gordon Childe is more cautious about a numerical estimate and confines his reference to groups of Neanderthal skeletons which evidently had ritual burial.[2]

The members of each group would necessarily have a common outlook and many common interests arising from the nature of their interdependence. Within the group itself familiarity would give rise to mutual toleration and even affection. The in-group code of ethics stresses kindliness, cooperation, and a brotherly spirit. A good member of a group is one who coordinates his per-

[1] Sir Arthur Keith, *A New Theory of Human Evolution* (New York: Philosophical Library, 1948), Essays I-VI.
[2] V. Gordon Childe, *Man Makes Himself* (New York: New American Library of World Literature, 1951), p. 50.

sonal activities with those of the other members, thereby promoting teamwork.

But the customary attitude toward individuals outside the group is in most instances precisely the opposite. Suspicion, hostility, and even enmity are the normal and approved modes of behavior toward the outsider.[3] The spirit of group solidarity demands and presumes such a viewpoint. Kindliness and toleration toward outsiders tends to weaken the group spirit, and is therefore usually accounted as traitorous and treasonable, particularly at times when the existence of the group is threatened.

Such a dual code of ethics is so common to all societies and at all stages of civilization that it may be termed a universal truth or principle. Even the higher animals frequently display such an attitude. A dog's behavior in his relations with the members of the family to which he belongs is radically different from his behavior toward strangers. Similarly, chimpanzees are quite hostile toward a strange member of their own species who may be thrust upon them.

On the assumption that the dual code of ethics is a universal principle among men, the development of civilization may be interpreted as a struggle between local loyalties and broader loyalties, wherein the in-group is conceived on an ever more comprehensive scale. As the loyalties grow broader and broader there is an increasing dependence upon intellectual perception, and a decreasing reliance upon purely emotional ties. As a consequence, the in-group spirit of affection and cooperation becomes watered down at the edges to mere toleration.

Each individual in a society appears to have a range or band of graduated tolerances. There are certain group affinities to which he merely pays lip service. He is extremely tolerant of deviations from the norm in these areas and is quite willing to consider in-

---

[3] Members of a group do not necessarily show hostility toward total strangers, as is evidenced by the behavior of the Australian aborigines toward white men. The hostility is aroused when a threat to the group becomes apparent.

tellectual arguments pro and con, regardless of whether the implications of such arguments undermine the group affinity or not. There are certain group affinities which he values highly, but he is willing to concede imperfections in them. He has a bias, but his mind is not closed to intellectual arguments. Finally, there are group affinities to which he clings passionately. The loyalty is cemented by powerful emotional ties which blind him to all rational arguments. Similarly, social groups appear to have such ranges or bands of tolerance.

Because local loyalties are strongly emotional, they come in the third category where little or no tolerance is shown toward deviations. As a result two basic problems arise. First, in order that a society may hold together, the broader loyalties must be kept more powerful than the local loyalties. Otherwise the interests of the society will be submerged by the interests of the local groups. Second, since the local loyalties are sustained largely through their appeal to the emotions, these loyalties are particularly resistant to change. Yet they do change over time, as history clearly shows. But how are the changes brought about?

In order to maintain strong broader loyalties and thus bring about cohesion within the society, man has had to evolve some technique so that the intellectual or rational forces are strengthened to the point where they can compete successfully with the more emotional and powerful local loyalties. Émile Durkheim has described this cohesive force which strengthens the broader loyalties as the *âme collective*. But, like many of his "social facts," this concept is distinctly metaphysical and therefore scientifically unacceptable.[4] The reinforcing technique is purely operational. It is manifested in the operational mediums or conveyances[5] which man has developed as part of both his material and mental cultural tradition.

By this interpretation change within the society comes about through alterations in the conveyances. For example, con-

[4] Durkheim's study of suicides is not metaphysical.
[5] These terms are defined later in the chapter.

sider the modern development of labor unions. They constitute a much more comprehensive and powerful conveyance than their predecessors, the trade unions, or even earlier, the guilds. The implications of modern labor unions for local loyalties among workers within given trades or geographical areas have been profound. Many former local loyalties have been so altered as a result of the new conveyance as to be almost unrecognizable.

Powerful conveyances serve to strengthen the broader loyalties. Yet, even when these conveyances operate sufficiently well to maintain a strong cohesive force within the society, the local loyalties continue to flourish in the form of sectional or vested interests within the larger framework. The scale and level of culture of a civilization, geographically, ethnically, and intensively, i.e., the amount of specialization, depends upon the degree of breadth of group spirit to which the civilization can respond as a cohesive unit. And, of course, the cohesion depends upon how well the conveyances function to maintain and strengthen the broader loyalties.

There appears to be a tendency for civilizations to continue their expansion until the conveyances become inadequate to support the broader and broader loyalties. The cohesive force is then weakened. When the point is reached where the local loyalties have become stronger than the broader loyalties, the civilization has become overexpanded and is in a state of disequilibrium.

Historically, succeeding civilizations[6] have attained ever higher and higher cultural levels, have developed better and better conveyances, and have grown in geographic extent, population, and ethnical groupings and in the degree of specialization and interdependence. But in every instance they have eventually reached a point where the conveyances failed to support the new broader loyalties adequately, and failed to maintain a sufficiently strong cohesive force. The local loyalties have become stronger than the broader loyalties; and internal disruption and conflict

[6] The term "civilization" as used here may be interpreted in the Toynbeean sense.

among the local loyalties have then brought about the decline and disintegration of that particular civilization.

It is notable that successor civilizations typically do not grow in the same area, nor are they developed by the direct descendants of the members of the parent civilization. A more primitive people, by borrowing from the older civilizations, build up new and superior conveyances which will help maintain broader loyalties and thereby develop a strong cohesive force. Meanwhile, the biological descendants of the older civilization cling to many of the outmoded rituals and customs, and become an insignificant group in the new order.

The characteristic life cycle of succeeding civilizations led nineteenth century social scientists into a false and misleading analogy between social cycles and biological cycles. A civilization was compared to a biological organism; the cycle of the civilization was considered to be similar to the biological cycle of birth, growth, maturation, reproduction, decay, and demise.[7] Modern sociologists have noted the erroneous nature of the analagy,[8] but have not so far developed the results of their findings to provide a schematic and convincing explanation which would establish causal factors.

Basic Assumptions

At this point it might be well to recapitulate by stating the basic assumptions upon which the argument thus far developed rests. Definitions of key terms have up to this point merely been implicit in the context. They should now be stated more formally. Then the steps toward the conclusions reached can be developed more fully.

The first assumption is that the evolution of human society has proceeded and continues to proceed through group forma-

[7] Herbert Spencer is the best known exponent of this analogy, although it is traceable also in the works of Auguste Comte and others.

[8] Kingsley Davis, *Human Society* (New York: The Macmillan Company, 1949).

tion. Second, the dual code of ethics enunciated by Keith is assumed to be an established social principle. Third, the development of succeeding civilizations on an ever grander, more eclectic, and more highly integrated form is noted as a historical datum. Fourth, inasmuch as the elapse of time since the beginning of civilization and written history is so brief, only 6,000 years or about 240 generations, it is reasonable to assume that modern man is little different biologically from neolithic man in the ancient cultures of Egypt, Mesopotamia, the Indus, or elsewhere. If we accept Keith's argument that biological change in man has probably slowed down with the progressive expansion in the size of the in-group, this assumption is thereby reinforced. Fifth, as a result of the fourth assumption, we are faced with the conclusion that the growth and development of succeeding civilizations on a progressive scale is purely cultural or social, and is the result of an accumulation of knowledge and of techniques through trial and error or experience.

But if this fifth and derived assumption is to be accepted, then why is it that some civilizations or successions of civilizations have advanced rapidly while others have developed with relative slowness? Also, why do the biological descendants of decaying civilizations fail to rebuild, while more primitive outsiders, by borrowing from the culture of these decaying civilizations, often succeed in building a new and more advanced successor civilization? To provide an adequate explanation for these phenomena a sixth assumption is needed. This assumption is that physical and mental conveyances are operative within human society. The implications of the sixth assumption are more complex and require a detailed exposition.

Conveyances

Lindesmith and Strauss in their study entitled *Social Psychology* describe the results of an experiment on a normal baby during the first year of his life. The sounds he made were recorded periodically.[9] It was found that the child by accidental occurrence had enunciated every known sound, consonant or syllable, used in any of the human languages—including the wonderful "l" sound of the Welsh language. Yet, we are all aware of the difficulty, sometimes almost insuperable, with which later in life we master unusual sounds in a foreign language.

A second experiment, this time in memory testing, was conducted with children of preschool age. In order to assist their memories, these children quickly learned to use numerous peculiar and often unique techniques of their own conception which would serve as a means of mental recall.[10] One child might arrange or cut out pieces of paper in a manner which had meaning for him or her alone. Another might use string as the instrument of record for later recall. Each worked out a system with available materials which functioned more or less adequately for the purpose. In continuing experiments each child continued to use the same technique he or she had originated, but with modifications or refinements developed through experience. Later, after these same children had attended school and had been taught the orthodox methods of recording, they were again tested. On this occasion not one of them used the technique he or she had originated; they all used the orthodox technique they had been taught.

The results of these experiments would appear to indicate that the original potentialities of the human mind are enormous and for all practical purposes immeasurable, since the mind is socialized and canalized at a very early age. They also indicate that the human mind seizes naturally upon definite means which will serve as a vehicle for the accomplishment of a desired end. Man is by his very nature a mental hitchhiker. He will use any and all means of conveyance, either physical or mental, to attain mastery over his environment. If he is forced to develop his own conveyances, his degree of success will be dependent upon three factors:

[9] A. R. Lindesmith and A. L. Strauss, *Social Psychology* (New York: The Dryden Press, 1949), pp. 137-139.
[10] *Ibid.*, pp. 86-87.

the cultural training he has received in the past, or to put it in another way, the mental equipment he brings to the problem; second, the physical environment, that is, the physical equipment or even potential equipment available; and third, his native intelligence. A fourth factor could well be the intensity of his desire, for the effort he will put forth is likely to be in direct proportion to the intensity of his interest.

Within the human group the individual goes through a triple form of development. As he approaches each new problem (1) he may push ahead and try to develop a technique to master it, or (2) he may be given the technique through cultural training before or as he comes to the problem, or (3) he may wait for or seek out the cultural training which will help him to meet the problem. The last course of action is in itself the result of cultural influence.

The individual learns to use materials and techniques, that is, physical or mental conveyances of his own manufacture plus those which he receives as a result of his cultural training. The proportion of each is likely to be determined by the nature of the society in which he lives. If the society is so organized that the individual is free to develop his own conveyances or even encouraged to do so, then an eclectic growth of culture is to be expected. If, on the other hand, the social organization is restrictive, the individual will be permitted little opportunity to develop original concepts and conveyances. Each extreme raises problems.

The ideal society insists that the individual members assimilate basic conveyances which are necessary for successful intercommunication and for the maintenance of both individual rights and responsibilities. But at the same time it creates a suitable environment and intellectual climate for individual formulation of new or modified conveyances which promote accomplishment and therefore societal welfare.

Such a society is more easily conceptualized than attained. It is never possible to predict the identity of the innovators, the timing of the innovations, or the form they will take. Consequently a wide measure of freedom to all members of the society is needed to promote maximum progress. Yet, in retrospect, we find that very few use the freedom to make a contribution of any sort. Moreover, a disturbingly large proportion regard their freedom as an inalienable right which entails no obligation to the society which grants it. In some instances the freedom is converted into license, thereby encouraging passionate local loyalties in a manner which endangers the broader loyalties.

We have so far indicated that the human mind relies upon physical and mental conveyances, that is, upon certain techniques or instruments, in order to formulate concepts which will help the individual to attain mastery over his environment. We have also noted that in any given society there will be certain well-established conveyances which all members use in common—with individual variations, of course. There will also be a periodic generation of new conveyances or variations of old conveyances by individuals within the society. The rate of such generation will be determined largely by the intellectual climate of the society in question. Some of these new conveyances or variations of old conveyances may be assimilated from time to time by the whole society, while others in current use may be dropped out.

A conveyance is an instrument or method which assists an individual or a group to attain an objective. First, there are physical conveyances. Not only men, but animals also, use features in the physical environment to their own advantage. The leopard uses the branch of a tree to hide above his prey. The fox uses a stream of water to throw the hounds off his trail. Moreover, animals are quite capable of altering the physical environment to suit their convenience. The bird uses grass and twigs to fashion a nest. The ground hog burrows out a sanctuary. But the animals receive comparatively little training. Most of the alterations are made instinctively. Man, on the other hand, alters his environment deliberately. If the method of constructing and of using a particular physical conveyance is forgotten by a society, it is irretrievably lost. It can be brought back into the culture through rediscovery only. Fortunately, a whole society rarely loses such knowledge completely. The method of staining glass was lost for a time, but has been worked out again. In that instance the method was lost but the use was not. The physical conveyances are the actual tools which man uses to alter his environment for a given purpose. Also, tools are made to make tools. The artist's palette, brushes, paints, and canvas are tools; but the finished painting is also a tool for the conveyance of an aesthetic concept. Physical conveyances, therefore, may be one or several times removed from the ultimate purpose of man. In the same way that compounded abstractions lead to greater ultimate mastery over a particular situation, so compounded physical conveyances result in improved material accomplishments. The modern era of capitalism is based on a system of multidegree conveyances. In other words, production is indirect, and highly efficient.

But behind each physical conveyance there must be a mental conveyance. When a monkey seizes a nut to hurl down on the beast of prey at the foot of the tree, he has conceived a system of attack through propulsion of objects. Primitive man goes much further. He conceives his weapons in advance of the time that he needs them. Foresight helps him to have greater command over the situation when it does arise. Similarly, by foresight man learns to prepare for the construction of tools which will in turn give him command over the future situation. The mental conveyances are pyramided in the same way as the physical conveyances.

One other type of conveyance has yet to be considered. This type might be termed the general conveyance. A tool, such as a saw or a hammer, can be used in the construction of many specific physical conveyances. Also, behind each general physical conveyance there must be a mental conveyance. But that mental conveyance is specific. It is a particular mental conveyance for the development of a general physical conveyance. The highest form of human thought is the general mental conveyance. And even general mental conveyances can be of the first, second, or higher degree. In other words, like all the others, general mental conveyances can be pyramided.

General mental conveyances are concepts or methods of thinking whereby specific mental conveyances can be developed. The scientific technique is a general mental conveyance. By using it the specific mental conveyances concerning nuclear fission were worked out. These in turn served to govern the development of the general and specific physical conveyances. Isotopes are a general physical conveyance, while the atomic bomb is a specific physical conveyance. A mathematical solution, such as the binomial theorem, is a general mental conveyance, but it is quite evidently on a lower order than the scientific technique. Yet it is a general mental conveyance, for it in turn provides the means for the development of certain specific mental conveyances which in their turn govern certain general as well as specific physical conveyances.

From the above set of definitions it is clearly evident that the use of the term "institution" to describe all of these aspects of physical and mental controls which man has over his environment is vague and inadequate. An institution is an established pattern of behavior. Consequently, any established conveyance could be called an institution, but the nomenclature would be misleading. This study is concerned primarily with the dynamic and not the established aspects of social life. The term "conveyance" emphasizes this fact.

The mental conveyances are definitely those of prime importance. One can easily conceive a society rebuilding physical conveyances which have been destroyed. But if a society should lose its mental conveyances, theoretically it would become completely primitive. Since the mental conveyances are not instinctive, but are passed from generation to generation through cultural training, the conveyances could be lost. Actually, however, there are so many means by which the culture is transmitted that a complete loss of mental conveyances could hardly be said to occur. Rather, there are periods during which many mental conveyances are retained by very few, and again periods during which the culture is spread among a greater proportion of the population. During the latter periods former generations also reach across to the contemporary students through the written word.

With physical conveyances there are two important factors to consider. First, there is the impact of the physical conveyance upon the human mind. In reaching for higher and ever higher abstractions upon which to build mental conveyances the human mind works from the concrete, physical reality to the abstract and thus to the theory. Existing physical conveyances, therefore, provide the means for further development. As an example, consider the use of numbers. The Egyptian numerical system was highly cumbersome, and consequently arithmetic solutions were extremely complex. General formulas were developed on a very limited scale. The Greeks, through the use of letters, were able to generalize much more satisfactorily. Similarly, the use of Roman numerals renders simple calculations particularly difficult, whereas the use of Arabic numerals and the decimal system encourages the development of mental conveyances. The nature of the physical conveyances of a society is quite evidently fundamental.

The second factor with respect to physical conveyances is their use by members of the society who have not mastered the mental conveyances which made the development of the physical conveyances possible. We readily appreciate the physical dangers involved when we permit mentally immature individuals to operate automobiles, but how well do we appreciate the devastating effects upon the society when political demagogues who do not understand the mental conveyances involved in a true definition of money presume to dictate monetary policies? The greatest danger to democracy is the damage which is wrought from within by individuals who exercise privileges which they are culturally incapable of handling to the best advantage of themselves and the society in which they live.

Loyalties

To complete this portion of the study into the eclectic causal theory, definitions for local loyalties and broader loyalties are needed. Probably, the simplest approach will be to define the adjectives "local" and "broader" first, and then proceed to the more complex term "loyalties." "Local loyalties" and "broader loyalties" are comparative terms. In a primitive society a local loyalty would be loyalty to one's tribe or totem, while a broader loyalty would be loyalty to a federation of tribes or to a deity shared by a group larger than the tribe. Among the Greeks loyalty to their own city-state was a local loyalty and loyalty to a federation of city-states was a broader loyalty. In modern times loyalty to a church denomination could be considered a local loyalty, while loyalty to a broad faith, such as Christianity, would be the broader loyalty. As a society becomes more highly cultured, the encompassing unit becomes larger and larger. As a result, loyalties which in a more primitive society were broader loyalties become local loyalties. As an example, consider the present-day attitude toward nationalism. Loyalty to the United Nations might be construed as the broader loyalty and loyalty to one's country as the local loyalty. In the European culture, loyalty to a proposed United States of Europe is the broader loyalty.

The term "loyalty" arises, of course, from the dual code of ethics discussed earlier. Loyalties are emotional, in contrast to mental conveyances, which are intellectual. Primarily, loyalty to a group of any sort entails identification of personal welfare with the welfare of that group. The loyalty is not instinctive, but rather is an identification of the loyalty with an instinctive desire. The Pharaohs of Egypt held the loyalty of their people because the Pharaohs were able to identify themselves, in the eyes of the people, with three fundamental human desires. First, the Pharaohs, by claiming divinity, provided their people with a common object of worship. Second, they provided the stability and security necessary for an agricultural form of community life. And third, by organization and direction the flood waters of the Nile were used to better advantage than had been possible under community direction. The religious, political, and economic ties were so powerful that the people unquestioningly identified their interests with the interests of the Pharaoh.

(As long as the group supplies the needs of the majority, loyalty to the group is assured.) Moreover, since the loyalty is identified with instinctive desire in one or several forms, the loyalty is blind to intellectual argument. Yet, since the loyalty itself is not the instinct, every loyalty is amenable to qualification and modification over time.

The qualification arises from the coexistence of a number of local loyalties. An individual is ordinarily a member of several groups simultaneously. Unduly burdensome demands of loyalty by one group are therefore restrained by the demands of other groups. No one of them can dominate completely. When a number of the loyalties are attached within a single grouping, then that grouping commands a disproportionately large amount of allegiance. It is less subject to qualification. The Pharaohs, because they dominated three of the major groupings, the religious, the political, and the economic, were able to exert an enormous influence. They commanded three loyalties. In the present-day society it is interesting to note that the Communist doctrine as promulgated by Russia is designed to amalgamate loyalties in the same way as the Pharaohs did. The Communist doctrine is basically materialistic and therefore economic. But it is notable that the doctrine also appeals to internationalism (or more properly today, Russian imperialism); moreover, a materialistic form of religion is manifest both in the doctrine of Karl Marx and in the utterances of contemporary Russian leaders.

Grouping of loyalties results inevitably in loss of individual freedom. As long as the loyalties are owed to different groups, no one of these groupings can make especially onerous demands of allegiance. (The demands of a particular group must always be tempered by the forms of allegiance which the members of the group owe to other groups in the society.) Consequently the individual emerges with a much larger measure of freedom. The division of loyalties has resulted in compromise and restraint which permits the intellectual aspects to gain a hearing.

Social Change

Modification of loyalties is more difficult to describe. Because the loyalties are not themselves instincts, modification over time, particularly over a period of several generations, is possible. The most powerful loyalties are extremely resistant to change, but even they undergo alteration over time. Loyalty to a particular religion is probably the most logic-tight form of loyalty. Yet old religions do pass away and new religions take their place, although many of the forms and rituals of the old religion find their way into the new. Man changes his loyalties, but finds it easier to do so when the change is insidious rather than overt. Only when the change-over has become long overdue does the modification become direct and violent.)

The original loyalty is built up because the individual members of the group sense that the group interest is also their interest. In other words, they identify the group interest with their instinctive desires. Once this occurs the contract becomes binding to a superlative degree. The individual members no longer think as individuals, but rather as members of the group. They have surrendered not only the right but also the ability to think for themselves as individuals. The social contract has become completely binding.

It is at this point that Montesquieu makes a serious error. He concludes that because the social contract is binding it must also be permanent. Members of a society who have been trained to think in a certain manner are emotionally and intellectually blind in their loyalties, it is true. But such emotional attachment to established loyalties varies among the individual members of the society. Also, each member attaches varying significance to the different loyalties which the society has built up. This point was mentioned earlier, when we spoke of loyalties to which some individuals pay lip service, loyalties to which they are attached but recognize as being imperfect to a greater or lesser degree, and loyalties to which they are blindly attached. Finally, the succession of generations is instrumental in bringing about an alteration in the amount of attachment to loyalties. The continuous flow of new individuals into the society and of old individuals from the society guarantees at least some measure of divergence and alteration in the interpretations over time.

On the other hand, the argument of Jean Jacques Rousseau that the social contract is made by man as an individual and may therefore be abrogated at will is quite as faulty as the diametrically opposite argument of Montesquieu.[11] In the first place, Rousseau assumed that primitive man in his natural state is a solitary creature, whereas all evidence is to the contrary. Man would not be manlike in other than a social environment. In a social environment man does not make completely individual choices even in purely personal matters. His thinking is always conditioned by social as well as physical influences. Therefore, even the original formulation of a social contract does not involve individual choice but rather an acceptance of decisions made by the dominant forces in that particular society. These dominant forces may be military, political, religious, economic, or a combination of them. The individual leaders of these dominant forces are themselves conditioned in their decisions and actions by social as well as physical environmental factors. To pursue this topic further would be to get into a theory of leadership with which this study is not directly concerned—although a study of religion and the role of leadership is long overdue.

Social conditioning is carried out in two ways. First, the mental conveyances of the individual are for the most part so-

[11] By "social contract" Rousseau meant "political contract." In this work the meaning is broadened to include all forms of social contract.

cially acquired. Consequently the actual processes by which the individual thinks are conditioned. Second, the society, because it is stronger than the individual, can coerce him into obedience to social contracts. Such coercion may range all the way from ridicule to social ostracism. In addition the society may place physical restrictions on recalcitrant individuals or mete out physical punishments. But the control over the mental conveyances is the most important means by which the individual is made to conform. The society must control the thinking of the vast majority if order is to be maintained. Physical coercion is useful in controlling the occasional malcontent only.

Yet, regardless of whether the society is highly restrictive or whether it is exceedingly tolerant of individual variations, some change in the social structure will occur over time. In the latter case, the change is more rapid; the society advances more quickly to higher levels of culture, and at the same time is always in danger of becoming more unstable, since cultural dissemination to permit widespread comprehension of abstractions involved in the new conveyances is racing to keep pace with the broader and ever broader loyalties which the higher levels of culture have thrust upon the society. During such periods of rapid progress, a smaller and smaller proportion of the members of the society are able to master the abstractions involved in the flood of new or modified conveyances, and therefore fewer and fewer members of the society respond adequately to the broader loyalties. The cultural lag between the intellectual leaders of the society and the general populace broadens. Those members of the society who do not master the abstractions involved in the new broader loyalties cling to the local loyalties which they can understand. As a result the cohesive force which binds the society together is weakened. The danger of disequilibrium grows.

Before proceeding to the consideration of motivations, the quality of conveyances should be discussed. Some societies develop conveyances which help them to gain a greater mastery over their physical environment than do others. The success with

which any society responds to its environment is directly dependent upon the quality and flexibility of the conveyances, and this
means the mental conveyances, in particular, which it has at its
disposal. A group may through superior fighting techniques attain mastery over others. But if it lacks adequate conveyances in
the other major areas of societal activity or fails to borrow and
adapt such conveyances quickly enough, its superiority is certain
to be short-lived. Societies which have developed the most successful conveyances in all the major fields are those which have
advanced the most rapidly in their culture, and which have passed
on to their successors the best-known forms for further development. The biological descendants of a successful civilization fail
at this point because they cling blindly to the old loyalties,
which in the new order have become local loyalties. These biological descendants are trained by their culture to look back and to
imitate rather than to seize upon useful features of the old culture
for emulation and adaptation to the new.[12]

Cultural Lags

A survey of the history of civilizations makes it clearly evident
that even the most successful civilizations up to the present have
all failed in some respects to develop fundamental conveyances
and thereby to strengthen the broader and ever broader loyalties
fast enough to perpetuate the civilization indefinitely. The cultural lags have widened.

There are two cultural lags. First, there is the lag between
the social sciences and the natural sciences. Six generations ago
Auguste Comte ventured the opinion that the Western culture
was then emerging from the metaphysical level to the positive or
scientific level. Contemporary society ordinarily takes it for
granted that it has taken this momentous step. But has it? In the
natural sciences such a claim is largely substantiated by physical
discoveries and inventions. But in the social and philosophical

[12] Descendants of the ancient Egyptians, Greeks, and Romans are examples.

realms contemporary thought is still for the most part metaphysical, and oftentimes even anthropomorphic. The notorious cultural lag between the natural sciences and the social sciences appears to have broadened.

Second, there is the cultural lag between the cultural leaders of a society and the general populace. If a society, such as that of the ancient Greeks, produces a few social philosophers far in advance of their times, is it to be accounted a mature society at the highest level, or must the level of thought of the general populace be taken into account? Both interpretations have a certain measure of validity. When the boundaries of human thought are explored, intellectual leadership is the criterion. But when the ultimate development of the society as a whole is taken into consideration, then the level of thought of the general populace becomes significant.

Also, longevity of a civilization is not necessarily correlated closely with successful conveyances. This brings us back to the problem of imbalance which occurs in a civilization when expansion has proceeded to the point where the degree of abstractions required for comprehension of the new conveyances is too great for the general populace, and where as a result the local loyalties are threatening to become stronger than the broader loyalties. A civilization which expands very little does not require such extremely complex conveyances, for even its broader loyalties are not very broad compared to those in the highly developed civilization. The cultural lag between the intellectual leaders and the general populace is not very large. Therefore, the civilization which has developed very little may be more stable and consequently longer-lived than the civilization which has greatly superior conveyances, but which has expanded to the point where one or both of the cultural lags have widened and where in consequence the abstractions of the general populace or the conveyances themselves are being strained in order to maintain the broader loyalties which have become necessary for the continuation of that civilization.

On the other hand, the less advanced civilization may suffer sudden demise when it meets outside forces which compel change. Such an outside force may be contact with a highly developed civilization, or possibly fundamental environmental changes as a result of physical factors. The underdeveloped civilization simply does not have the higher-level conveyances which will carry the broader loyalties now forced upon it.[13]

In tracing the course of a civilization, therefore, the pertinent factors are, first, the nature of the conveyances at its disposal, and, second, the amount of expansion which is attempted or which the civilization is forced to attempt as a result of outside forces.

At the primitive level a society may endure indefinitely even though its mental and physical conveyances are equally primitive, so long as they are sufficient to cope with the broader loyalties needed for group cohesion. When the primitive society develops and expands it must improve its conveyances in order to maintain strong broader loyalties. The quality of the conveyances must be improved; also, a system must be devised whereby the mental laggards in the society are either coerced by mental and physical restraints or else educated so that they will support the broader loyalties. As the conveyances become more abstract and as the broader loyalties expand in size and in extent, emotional ties are weakened. The newly formed civilization must learn to rely more upon intellectual appeals in order to maintain group solidarity. This is always the primary weakness in any advanced civilization. But the broader loyalties are not dependent entirely upon intellectual appeals. Through persuasion, symbols, slogans, and other devices (which are various forms of vulgarization) emotional ties can be brought in to strengthen the broader loyalties.

A civilization may crumble as a result of failure to modify and

---

[13] The civilization of the Incas provides an example of sudden demise through contact with an outside force. The native Negro societies are tougher. They have met the challenge of the white man's culture in two ways, first, by excluding it wherever possible, and second, by assimilating conveyances where necessary.

to develop existing conveyances rapidly enough to cope with the broader loyalties which are growing in size and complexity as a result of expansion. Or it may crumble through a lack of conveyances which can be modified and developed to deal with the problem. Or it may crumble as a result of deterioration of the conveyances, i.e., rigidifying of religious dogma or persistent debasement of the monetary system. In any case, the local loyalties ultimately become stronger than the broader loyalties, the group cohesion is weakened, and the civilization collapses of its own weight—such collapse being hastened, no doubt, by the external pressures which are always present.

The successor civilization may succeed where its predecessor failed: (1) by introducing the necessary modifications to the existing conveyances so that they will cope with the broader loyalties now needed, or (2) by introducing new fundamental conveyances which can be modified to cope with these broader loyalties. Usually the successor civilization uses a combination of these two alternatives. Moreover, the new fundamental conveyances or the modifications to the old may be original with the successor civilization, or they may have been borrowed in turn from other cultures. Again a combination of these two alternatives is likely to occur.

Motivations

We have now come to what is probably the most important part of the eclectic causal theory, namely, the study of motivations. We noted that over time change does come about with respect to both the conveyances and the loyalties, even the blind loyalties. But what influence brings about this change? We are aware of influences wrought by the geographic environment. But, in addition to the nonhuman influences, the human beings within the society itself are motivated to seek change.

Three motivations stand out among all others. The first is the intellectual urge of superior individuals in the society to build up higher forms of abstractions and theory. The second is the cataclysmic scurry for new conveyances and new loyalties when long overdue adjustments are made, so that the society can deal with changes which have already insidiously occurred and which up to this point have been ignored. This sudden change is often referred to as "the crisis theory of change." The third is the theory of the middle class. Suppose we examine each of these motivating factors in turn. When integrated they form a composite theory of social change.

Intellectual motivation is the simplest and at the same time the most baffling aspect of social change. Because man is social and a creature of habit, he adheres in his everyday conduct to rather set forms of behavior. Moreover, being more physical than mental—or to put it in another way, being mentally indolent—he prefers to follow precedent where possible instead of devising new methods.[14] Yet, in spite of these proclivities, man does create new mental and physical forms which result in change.

Just as a child engages in block building for the pleasure of the action, man engages in mental block building from sheer mental exuberance. Among uncultured peoples the activity is almost entirely sporadic and is rarely productive. If the customs of the society discourage change, the new forms are likely to be concentrated in special areas, such as dancing, pottery forms and ornamentation, personal attire, storytelling, music, or other cultural activities where some variation is usually permissible. Even these activities are often largely stereotyped in static societies. Chinese art is an example. Pottery forms and markings are also often characteristic for a given culture. But, even in the most static forms of human society, some variation in a few of these areas will occur. The variations are the result of mental block building or experimentation, and this block building is in turn a direct result

---

[14] This is not to deny the utility and necessity of habit. Many social actions are habitual to the point where they become acquired reflexes. Indeed, for most social intercourse we must be able to count on the behavior of others under given circumstances.

of man's proclivity to speculate concerning physical phenomena and his own place in the physical universe.

Such creative activity is not necessarily haphazard. It may occur as a result of deliberate effort. Once this stage is reached, the creator becomes a researcher. He may or may not find what he seeks, but his efforts will very likely bring about discovery of some sort. Also, the findings will more probably be productive, since pragmatic considerations will now be of importance. Moreover, a new motivation, never entirely absent, becomes evident. The researcher desires the recognition of the society, and therefore endeavors to prove the worth of his research. In its purest form research may be motivated by a desire for mastery over physical environment, but social influences are an important factor also. They represent the pragmatic aspect of the motivation.

In general, the intellectual urge for discovery of and mastery over the forces of nature constitutes the motivation for pure or basic research. Pure researchers are theoreticians of the highest order, delving into the most obscure places for knowledge, building highly complex sets of abstractions to improve their comprehension and detailed understanding of the physical phenomena being studied. It is quite conceivable that pure researchers can be entirely independent of a social motivation—though proof of this would be hard to establish. Spinoza was content to leave his greatest work unpublished in his lifetime, but that does not prove that he was not influenced by a desire for social recognition by posterity. The intellectual urge is undoubtedly a factor in bringing about change, but it is not an unalloyed factor which can be reduced to terms of complete simplicity any more than pure or basic research can ever be completely divorced from applied and developmental research. The pragmatic factor is sometimes kept within reasonable bounds, but it is never entirely absent.

The crisis theory of change has many proponents and is interpreted in numerous ways. For the most part, however, it is portrayed as a purely social phenomenon. Once we assume that

creative activity, either haphazard or deliberate, does occur in a society, the stage is set for periodic crises. Such crises may occur, of
course, as a result of physical changes over which man has no control. Glacial ages, earthquakes, tidal waves, and tornadoes are examples. But many of the physical alterations are traceable to
human influence. Soil erosion through wasteful means of cultiva-
tion is a prime instance. Some geographic determinists consider
that the ultimate destruction of the Mesopotamian civilizations
is directly attributable to this latter factor. But the Nile floods
did not fail, and yet the Egyptian civilization died out. Geographic determinism provides a partial explanation, but too much
reliance upon it blinds us to other and equally important factors.

In the society a process of intellectual development proceeds
spontaneously but at varying rates and at various levels of deliber-
ation. Through this process improved abstractions and superior
conveyances (mostly mental and highly generalized) are continu-
ously being generated. But the process is itself purely an incuba-
tion growth. It can and frequently does occur in semi-isolation
from the society as a whole. During periods of staticism in the
society the reservoir of intellectual comprehension is slowly built
up. Then, when the society is faced with a series of crises, recourse is had to this reservoir of abstractions.[15] Developmental
and applied research now proceeds rapidly, feeding on the results
of the pure research. The highly generalized mental conveyances
form the basis for a flood of specific mental conveyances and general as well as specific physical conveyances.

As long as the generation of the general mental conveyances
proceeds fast enough to meet the demand for developmental and
applied research, the conveyances are altered and improved to
meet the needs of the progressive society. But the first cultural
lag eventually broadens. The conveyances in the natural sciences
are developed so rapidly that the conveyances in the social sci-

[15] The pragmatic research in America today finds its roots in the pure
research of Copernicus, Galileo, Francis Bacon, and other Renaissance
thinkers.

ences are inadequate to cope with the challenges which the society now faces. In Toynbee's phraseology, the responses to these challenges or crises become more and more feeble, and to meet the problem the society reverts finally to authoritarianism. The second cultural lag, that between the cultural leaders and the general populace, is also operative in promoting this development. The response thus takes the form of restraint upon further social progress, and a lengthy period of deliberate and enlightened staticism ensues.

The static period permits the reservoir of general abstractions to be built up. It also permits the two cultural lags to narrow somewhat once again. But a new influence now becomes operative, and ultimately brings about the disintegration of that particular civilization. This influence is privilege. Development of further general mental conveyances is stifled. The intellectual climate is no longer conducive to individualistic and independent thought. The ubiquitous and choking influence of privilege places a limit on the ultimate peak of culture which that society can hope to attain. When this peak is reached the recurrent crises which come thereafter are left unresolved, save by further restraint. The restraints build up internal pressures which are again restrained until the point is reached where the uneasy equilibrium is dissipated and the societal structure disintegrates in a series of breakdowns.

The crisis theory of change, it will be noted, provides a splendid description of what occurs during the development and disintegration of a society. Yet it is essentially a descriptive and not an explanatory theory. It traces a societal process which we can observe historically, but the prime motivating forces within the process remain unexposed. The intellectual motivation did tell us something of the causal factors in connection with the development of conveyances. But for an adequate interpretation the loyalties need to be taken into account also. In addition the societal interplay between conveyances and loyalties requires consideration. This brings us finally to the theory of the middle class.

A barbaric society is characterized by a pyramidal social formation, wherein a few at the top dominate the many at the lower levels. A more meaningful analogy is to picture the societal structure as a collection of aggregative units each possessing certain attractive or cohesive and certain repelling or disintegrative powers. At the base of the pyramid the units are packed closely together, and form a unitary mass in themselves. They are held in this position partly by cohesive attraction and partly by the repelling quality of the units nearer the summit of the pyramid. In the early barbaric form of a civilization the pyramid is well filled at the top and bottom but is singularly empty in between. From time to time, however, certain more restless segments of the aggregative units at the bottom break away from the mass and thrust their way upward. As soon as they do break away they are subject to a number of simultaneous and conflicting forces. The aggregative units at the bottom exert both an attractive force and a repelling force, that is, an attractive force so long as the segments are still close to the aggregation and a repelling force when the pieces have through their internal dynamic powers moved a certain distance above the aggregation of bottom units. Meanwhile the topmost units exert a strong repelling force which prevents these segments from moving upward very far. Consequently the restless segments tend to find a position somewhere between the top and the bottom.

The segments themselves, which may be atomistic (individuals) or agglomerative (groups of individuals), often group together to form new aggregative units. But such units, unlike the more stable top and bottom units, are always in a state of activity, and the individual components exhibit a high degree of independence in their movements. They desert one unit to join a higher one very easily. These middle and highly restless aggregative units seek always to overcome resistance from above and thus to move higher in the pyramid. Sometimes they, or individuals among them, actually do succeed in overcoming the resistance. This may be done by forceful means or by more insidious means whereby the repelling force from above is deflected sufficiently to provide a pathway upward.

Once an individual or an aggregative unit in the middle area does succeed in reaching the top, it immediately joins forces with its new associates in pushing the others down. Moreover, if a topmost unit loses position it is thrust downward.

Finally, the aggregative units within the pyramid are always attached together by tenuous connections. Through these connections sustenance for the upper units is drawn from the base units, and these in turn draw this sustenance from the primary source, the earth beneath. The function of the lower units is thus to provide the sustenance; the function of the middle units is to improve the system, although they often create disorder in the process; and the function of the top units is to maintain order within the system.

Such is the purely mechanistic interpretation of the societal structure. The structure can also be described in terms of loyalties and conveyances, and a description couched in these terms is probably more explanatory. The loyalties for the in-groups constitute the cohesive force which holds each aggregative unit together, while the hostility to the outsider constitutes the repelling force. Similarly groups of the aggregative units have loyalties which draw them together into clusters, and over all the clusters certain broad loyalties hold the entire structure in place. The conveyances constitute the connecting links among the individuals within each aggregative unit, among the units, and among the clusters of units. The restive individuals and groups of individuals are engaged always in breaking down old loyalties, altering and improving conveyances, and ultimately building up new loyalties. They do this incidentally in their individual and collective efforts to rise to a higher level in the social scale. When many of these restless elements are active the society is dynamic. It is changing in its formation and in general is improving its organization and system; but the process of change is upsetting to the stability of the entire structure. In fact, if the change becomes too rapid, so that maladjustments multiply, the existence of the entire structure becomes endangered. Yet the conditions for stability tend ultimately to prevail. A society is not likely to disintegrate because of the energizing element. The emotional factor, that is, the loyalties, reasserts control before that happens, and restraints are again imposed which restore stability. The ultimate decline and disintegration occur eventually, not because of too much activity but rather because of too little activity—that is, because of rigidities arising from inertia and parasitical privilege. Slow growth of maladjustments through adherence to old conveyances and old loyalties which fail to meet the requirements of the new conditions eventually brings about the disintegration. At such times the energizing elements have been so restrained that they have died out. It is notable that in the final stages of the disintegration not only do the existing conveyances deteriorate rapidly, but also even the local loyalties are endangered. Privilege and restriction have proceeded to where the societal structure can no longer hold together. But this aspect of the total problem is not important for this study.

The Theory of the Middle Class

The theory of the middle class now becomes clear. Members of the middle class are individualists who seek to break down old loyalties so that they as individuals can gain entry into groups of a higher standing. The middle class individualist may do this by overt action, that is, by direct force. In that event the attack is sudden, violent, and quickly resolved. If he succeeds the successful middle class individualist moves into the preferred group and immediately sheds his role as a rule breaker. He now becomes a defender of privilege, and thereby ceases to be middle class. Militaristic conquerors are only briefly iconoclastic. Ordinarily they are upholders rather than breakers of tradition. Unsuccessful conquerors also quickly revert to inaction.

The true middle class individualist is one who uses insidious means to gain entry into preferred groups. Since the insidious method is time consuming, the individualistic characteristics assume more lasting form and significance. These individuals become the yeast in the society. By their fermenting action they alter the conveyances (borrowing their ideas from the pure or basic researchers), modify loyalties by qualification or other indirect means, coalesce loosely among themselves for collective action, and generally induce change in the society.

Middle class individualists may be active in any form of societal organization, religion, politics, economics, warfare, education, the arts, or even philosophy. They all seek recognition, and in their efforts to get such recognition they bring about innovations. They are the applied and developmental researchers, not through choice but through necessity. By altering the societal structure they gain their ends. They are complete pragmatists and justify their actions accordingly.

Since the middle class individualist is most likely to gain his ends through material success, he is perhaps most evidently active in the economic sphere. Therefore in developing the theory of the middle class we shall concentrate on the economic aspects of societal structures. This does not mean that middle class individualists are not active in the other fields, but rather that the theory is most easily developed by using the economic interpretation. The study which follows thus becomes a unitary causal theory. It explores society from one viewpoint. By compounding such studies a many-sided interpretation can eventually be developed which would be, of course, less biased. Perhaps ultimately the many-sided interpretation thus obtained could be formulated into one great and more or less complete eclectic causal theory.

But for the present we must restrict our view somewhat in order to get a clearer picture, fully appreciating that the deliberate restriction will bring about a materialistic bias.

CHAPTER TWO

Early Economic Organization

Assumptions

The six basic assumptions outlined in Chapter One form the foundation upon which the present theory of the middle class is constructed. The actual development of the theory, however, presumes a detailed analysis of the internal organization of social groups. A seventh assumption is therefore necessary at this time in order to clarify the terms of the analysis. It is assumed that men are not biologically equal or identical either mentally or physically. They are similar in contrast to other members of the animal kingdom, and they have certain attributes in common—the most striking being the curvature of the spine, the arch of the foot, the contraposition of the thumb, and a large cranial capacity. But the most fundamental characteristic of man is his ability to interpret arbitrary symbols. He alone among the members of the animal kingdom is capable of such interpretation, and consequently he alone is capable of abstract conceptualization. Nevertheless, among themselves men do not share this ability equally. Moreover, there are differences in physical structure, in various mental aptitudes, and in emotional balances.

This seventh assumption of inequality and dissimilarity does not necessarily extend to ethnical superiority. Except in a few

instances, such as with the African pygmies or the Australian
aborigines, there is no convincing evidence that one race of mankind, or one subrace of man, is definitely superior or inferior to all
others. Any suggestion of ethnocentrism is to be avoided as
scientifically unsound.

But with this important qualification in mind, differences
among individuals within social groups or between social groups
may be recognized. However much the differences may be due to
biological factors, and however much they may be due to cultural
factors, the differentiation itself may be accepted as factual.

Primitive Groups

Thorstein Veblen argued that in the primitive society, because
the "predatory instinct" in the male is normally stronger than in
the female, a patriarchal form of society was customary.[1] Sociologists through functional and historical studies have established
that primitive forms of society are and have been highly diverse.
Yet it is notable that even in the matriarchal societies the male
relatives of the wives have normally been in control—the difference being that these male relatives instead of the husband
wielded the power. Even he was an influential member of his own
tribe when he returned to it, which was apparently with fre-
quency.

The division of labor in the primitive society, while subject
to wide variation, was typically a matter of honor. The male engaged in the honorable occupations, which included fighting, play
fighting or contests, care of arms, hunting, fishing, religious exercises, and government. He did not ordinarily engage in monoto-
nous activities or tasks which entailed drudgery. In the matter of
consumption the situation was quite the reverse. The male members of the group, being in a position of authority, were naturally

[1] Thorstein Veblen, *The Theory of the Leisure Class* (originally pub-
lished in 1899; New York: Modern Library, n.d.), Chap. i.

the favored consumers. What they did not want or need then went to the women and children. This far we may follow Veblen's theory; but now we must leave it to explore in another direction.

In the primitive group no system of exchange among the members of the group was necessary. Save for very incidental items, private property did not exist. Nominally ownership was vested in the head of the family or in the chieftain of the group, but such ownership was simply a property right in trust. The head of the family or the chieftain of the group was responsible for the distribution of the production among the individual members. And as we have noted above, both the division of labor and the system of distribution were determined largely by family or tribal status rather than by individual choice or merit. No doubt, natural aptitudes, skill, and training each played a part in the final analysis, but only within narrow limitations. The broad categories of labor and of distribution were set by the status of the individual within the family and of the family within the tribe.

Ruler-Slave Society

With the formation of early states a profound change took place. In the primitive society the social disparity between the chieftain and the most insignificant member of the tribe was never very great. Close association and biological connection both operated to strengthen the emotional ties, so that the division of labor and the system of distribution were always fairly reasonable. But with the formation of civilized states the disparity began to increase in magnitude. The successful chieftain now became a king, surrounded by powerful nobles, a priestly class and men-at-arms. A distinct ruling class came into existence, and with its emergence there came into being by contrast a slave population.

The slaves probably developed as an underprivileged class through conquest, as the small groups warred upon each other and thus brought about the formation of the state.[2] In the ancient cultures a conquered people had no status whatsoever. In the eyes of the conquerors the lives of the vanquished were really forfeit, and were spared only that the conquered peoples might be used as instruments of production in the same way that animals are used. The head of the family in the primitive group might regard his wife or wives and children somewhat in the light of chattels, but never quite as slaves without rights or privileges of any sort.

A simple ruler-slave state could and probably did for a time exist without any form of money. The slaves produced and the rulers consumed. But the complexities of the larger organization raised problems of exchange. Moreover, exchange with individuals and groups outside the state were certain to occur more frequently and on a greater scale than had taken place among the primitive groups. A system of trading by barter inevitably resulted. Similarly some slave populations engaged in certain semi-independent occupations, such as farming, were ordinarily required to pay tribute or taxes on the resultant production in the form of commodities. Transfer of commodities either as a result of barter or in payment of taxes necessitated some system of measurement, no matter how crude it might be. Certain commodities in universal demand, such as slaves or cattle or gold rings, might serve in a very limited way as a medium of exchange, although they were probably more commonly used as a reference for measurement.[3]

As with primitive groups, private property on a very restricted scale existed in early societies, but complete and impersonal control of private wealth which accompanies ready convertibility was not present. Most forms of wealth were not negotiable. A king or noble who ruled a kingdom or owned an estate had quite as many obligations as he had privileges. He had to

    [2] James Henry Breasted, *A History of Egypt* (New York: Charles Scribner's Sons, 1912), p. 47. Also G. Steindorff and K. C. Seele, *When Egypt Ruled the East* (Chicago: The University of Chicago Press, 1942), pp. 1-12.

    [3] James Henry Breasted, *The Conquest of Civilization* (New York: Harper & Brothers, 1926), p. 75.

provide protection for himself and for the inhabitants, which meant that he could not split up the kingdom or estate without endangering its safety. He was the current incumbent only, and was more or less obliged to pass the possession along intact to his successor.

This type of family ownership extended not only to land, improvements, and livestock, but also to human beings since slavery was a normal part of the economic organization. Ownership or, more properly, overlordship, of a portion of land presumed complete control and ownership of all that lay within the territorial boundaries of the tract—buildings, equipment, livestock, and human beings. This was not merely a feudal arrangement peculiar to medieval Europe; in one form or another it permeated all ancient civilizations.[4] Complex systems of caste and social status marked the more advanced societies of ancient times, but all had a common formation as an outgrowth of conquest which broke down the primitive tribal groupings.

Secular and Religious Leaders

At the head of each society came the secular and religious leaders. The secular leader, clothed always in a religious aura, typically would be surrounded by his immediate family and by a group of high-ranking nobles, each in individual possession of large estates. Blood ties and cultural similarity welded the secular ruler and his nobles into a fairly compact unit.[5] If the state was warlike the secular ruler was more likely to grant his men-at-arms a fairly important degree of status. The soldier caste would then form a group below the nobility but above the common herd. In religious societies or where knowledge and refinement ranked high, as in China, the soldiers would more likely be mere mercenaries with little social prestige.

Religious leaders also formed a small and compact unit, closely

[4] *Ibid.*, p. 85.
[5] Breasted, *A History of Egypt*, p. 77.

allied by family bonds to the secular authority. Ordinarily the
supreme office of high priest carried less open authority than
that of the secular ruler. There were two reasons for this limitation. First, the secular authority was a controlling factor; but
second, and even more important, was the religious entity or
entities which formed the basis for the creed. The priests ostensi-
bly acted in the role of intermediaries and interpreters for the
common people. Even the high priest was always overshadowed
by the supreme authority which he only purported to represent.
He held his power primarily by virtue of his office and only sec-
ondarily as an outstanding individual. Church authority, therefore, tended to be oligarchical while secular authority was monarchical.

Church authority was nonetheless powerful. It acted
through its control over the human emotions. By canalizing these
emotions into suitable channels, it maintained implicit and un-
questioning obedience to spiritual authority. The formal church
was the repository of all official knowledge. It performed, with religious significance, the economic rites which accompanied mundane activities, such as the spring festival to accompany seeding
operations, the harvest festival, equinoctial and summer or win-
ter solstice observations, the coming or passing of rainy seasons, or
floods. Allied to each rite were the practical operations, such as
remeasurement of land after floods, as in Egypt, the measurement of time as with the solstice, or the official records of vital
statistics, as with marriage consecration or funeral rites. Any extraordinary economic activities also required religious sanction.
Warlike activities, marauding, and commercial voyages were accompanied by sacrificial observations and thanksgiving apportion-
ments.

Whichever predominated, secular and church authorities
were always closely interwoven and mutually interdependent.
Between them control was maintained by a few over the numerous slaves and semislave peasantry. But neither form of absolute

authority could deal forever with the insidious influence of new forms of wealth—particularly portable and negotiable wealth.

Formation of a Middle Class

In primitive societies there had been only a simple division of labor within the family groups. A broader division could and no doubt did occur in early civilizations without disturbing the ruler-slave caste system. Even the art of writing fitted into the religious and to a more limited extent the secular organization without disturbing the completely authoritarian form of government. But as the civilizations developed, the more complex division of labor created new problems and demanded new solutions which were eventually to alter the very basis of these civilizations. For how does a complex division of labor arise? What makes this form of societal life possible, and what encourages its development? The answer, of course, is negotiable wealth— money.

Money is portable and negotiable wealth—or an acceptable representation thereof. Its ownership is peculiar to the possessor alone. He may keep it, divide it up, or dispose of it in exchange for other forms of wealth at will. Private ownership no doubt existed before money, but it was not personal, that is, purely individual ownership in this new sense. Previous to the use of the money conveyance there was no true individualism. Each member of the society held a definite position in it on the basis of social status, which was usually determined by family connections. An individual was rarely a person in the truly singular sense, but rather a member of a given family, of a given social caste, of a given group. His personal possessions, if any, were but a part of the status and attached to him as privileges or responsibilities. But with money, that is, with portable and transferable wealth of any sort, mere possession added a new significance and provided a new status.

As an example, consider one of the dynamic forces which may

have been at work. Certain slaves, probably the more intelligent and personable ones, were from time to time relieved of their productive activities in order to act as household servants for their masters. The lot of these favored few was immeasurably better than that of the ordinary slaves. Through proximity with the luxury commodities being used in consumption they were certainly able to get their share. There has yet to be found the servant who does not benefit in kind in one form or another from his master. Because of their superior intelligence and culture these servant slaves were well equipped to benefit from their favorable environment. Items of portable wealth inevitably came into their possession from time to time and stayed there. As they attained wealth they assumed a new status. There was always the possibility that they might buy their freedom, or might desert their masters with some hope of successful escape, since they could take with them portable wealth with which to command services and status among strangers. Even if they remained as nominal slaves their increasing status placed them in a distinct class by themselves.

Thus we have the rise of a new class of individuals within the society. This class constituted individuals who were not to be ranked as slaves or peasants and yet not as rulers or overlords. They depended for their status upon continuous ownership of portable wealth. A middle class had been formed.[6] It is perhaps desirable to examine the necessary qualifications of a typical middle class person. He is by nature nonbelligerent; otherwise, with his superior intelligence, he would gravitate toward the ruling class. He is intelligent, shrewd, and highly rational; otherwise he would have remained a slave. He is strictly an individualist, dependent upon his rational powers for continued status. And because he is a rational individualist he accumulates wealth—preferably portable wealth.

An individual with portable and negotiable wealth might use it to pay for relief from social obligations. Thus, not only might a

[6] *Ibid.*, p. 85.

slave purchase freedom, but a peasant might buy privileges from his overlord, or a conscriptee might buy relief from military service. More complex divisions of labor were now facilitated and encouraged, whereby a tradesman, professional worker, or merchant could trade his wares or services for transferable wealth, and with it purchase his needs. A whole new class of individuals had come into existence. Money had become the catalyst whereby social change was being wrought.

The middle class picked up recruits from all directions until it came to include the professionals, the scribes, the merchants, some craftsmen, the traders, and the taxgatherers. Even the junior priests and men-at-arms were often included, although such members did not ordinarily share the peculiar mental characteristics of the others. These individuals could exchange their services on a limited scale by barter; but the use of portable and transferable wealth led inevitably to the selection of a nonperishable, compact, and divisible medium of exchange.[7] Even when not actually used in a transaction, money served as a measure or standard of value to which the traded items could be referred. Privileges, status, and physical possessions which formerly had not ordinarily been traded now assumed a commercial significance. But monetary status itself was the important element.

The possessor of commercial wealth did not fit into the old organization. As the owner of desirable and exchangeable utilities he had certain privileges and a special rating. But since he lacked exact authoritarian status linked with the state or the church, he was without a definite and assured position. Consequently, he tended to settle into an uneasy position between the lower classes and the overlord. Through money the middle class was born, devoid of specific authority or rank, but likewise free of responsibility and family status. Each member of the middle class was an individual dependent upon his own skill and shrewdness for continued societal position and freedom.

The existence of such a class of individuals presumes social and

[7] This was "electrum."

mechanical change. Each member of the middle class, dependent upon his instinct for combinations for societal survival and strongly individualistic in his objectives, was ever alert to develop and exploit new forms of wealth creation. The division of labor in the total society inevitably became more complex, while restrictive forms of state and religious authority were constantly being undermined by the insidious new influence. The search for wealth was quite as much a search for social status by nonbelligerent means. The ancient civilizations, such as Egypt, Sumeria, and even Babylonia, did not progress much beyond the creation of the middle class. Political instability which resulted in frequent reversion to the decision of force, coupled with general metaphysical forms of thought and a nonscientific approach, precluded very much development of middle class rationalism. It will be of interest, therefore, to trace briefly the fortunes of this incipient middle class in the earliest civilizations. Factual material is extremely scanty but there is enough available to glimpse something of the varying fortunes of this new group within the society, and thereby to deduce certain general principles concerning middle class characteristics, limitations, and potentialities.

CHAPTER THREE

The Incipient Middle Class

Social Requirements for a Middle Class

While there are numerous factors which will affect the progress and prosperity of a middle class, five of them stand out as being of fundamental importance. In the first instance a middle class cannot develop until there is a centralized government which is strong enough to maintain a reasonable degree of law and order in the trading area. A middle class depends upon its government for the provision of an arena in which trade and commerce can be carried on in a rational and nonbelligerent manner. The size of the arena will help to determine the extent of the growth of the middle class, for it also determines the extensive degree of specialization and division of labor which can be attained. Nevertheless, the middle class can to a limited extent push out past the actual boundaries of the centralized government's mandate, but such expansion of the trading arena will depend upon how much military support the middle class can expect from its home government in enforcing satisfactory trade regulations throughout this peripheral area, or how much stability of government and toleration already exist in these foreign sections.

Typically, these middle class excursions which are for rational reasons, that is, for profit, often form the basis for later imperial ambitions of home governments. It might be argued with some reason that one of the dynamic influences created by the middle class is the tendency to expand arenas of operation, which in turn leads to an ever-expanding size of states. A small state is encouraged to expand through imperialistic conquest in order to maintain adequate control over the peripheral areas on which it has become partly dependent for economic needs. The larger unit, after assimilation, becomes the new state. New imperialism then proceeds upon a vaster scale; and so the economic infiltration and expanding process continues, interrupted by periodic breakdowns of individual states and societies, but continuing in the long run regardless of such interruptions.

A second factor of fundamental importance for the development of a middle class is a reasonable measure of political and religious toleration. If the caste system is so rigid and so militaristic or so completely religious in form that rational behavior is stifled, very limited progress can be expected. Normally such restriction is temporary, and gradually gives way to moderation as the government becomes established firmly. Yet, some states such as Egypt, Assyria, and Sparta or, in modern times, Spain and possibly Germany are more warlike or religious than others and consequently permit little latitude to the middle class.

Other states, such as Phoenicia, its colony, Carthage, the Aegeans, and, in medieval times, the city-states of Italy, have been precisely the opposite. They were commercial states in which the middle class was granted the widest latitude. The middle class in each case operated almost exclusively in the peripheral areas, and depended upon sufficient stability of foreign governments to permit the continuation of trade. When such freedom disappeared, or when the home government was threatened, these states lacked the cohesive element necessary for survival. In the final analysis their instability lay in the fact that the military or religious forces in these states were too weak to maintain other broader loyalties and the necessary strength against outside forces. Too little latitude appears to stifle middle class action, therefore, while too much latitude appears to weaken other forces in the society which in turn break down the strong centralized government needed for stability.

A third factor, which stems from the first two, is the need for a limitation of warfare to areas outside the home territory. Warfare itself can stimulate middle class growth, so long as it is imperialistic warfare and is successful. Such warfare does not disturb activities in the main trading areas, and it opens up new areas for commercial exploitation. Warfare in the home territory, however, affects middle class activity unfavorably in two ways. First, it causes a breakdown or partial breakdown of commerce and trading, and, second, it results in more restrictive governmental measures as the military forces become extremely dominant.

A fourth fundamental factor in the development of the middle class is an adequate but stable form of money. The money conveyance must be adequate to permit a freely flowing stream of exchange of both goods and services. In this way specialization of labor is encouraged, rational behavior predominates, and economic wealth of all kinds is rendered more liquid and therefore enters more easily into the commercial arena; moreover, the caste system within the society is weakened, thereby allowing a greater measure of individual freedom. On the other hand, the money must be reasonably stable. If it fluctuates too drastically either up or down the terms of trade are thereby profoundly disturbed. If the prices are persistently forced downward by a failure to develop a monetary system that can keep pace with expansion of trade, then further expansion is discouraged. The liquidity preference chronically is high. If, on the other hand, the monetary system is persistently debased, as happened in Rome under the emperors, Gresham's law operates to drive out good money, and the monetary system then becomes unstable and inadequate. In this case the liquidity preference for the good money is too high and for the debased money too low.

A fifth factor of great importance to the growth of a middle class is adequate transportation. Specialization and division of labor, of course, presume movement of commodities over a wider area and consequently a cheap and efficient transportation system is imperative. To some extent natural advantages, such as a navigable river or nearness to the sea, are important factors; but if the first four factors are favorable the middle class is likely to alter physical transportation conditions radically to suit its purpose. The transportation factor, then, while absolutely necessary, is subject to a certain measure of modification under otherwise favorable conditions.[1]

With these factors in mind an examination of some of the very early civilizations will serve to show why in all instances the growth of the middle class was incipient. Some of these civilizations were more favorable areas for middle class development than others, but, until we come to the Greeks, each of them lacked certain necessary influences for a full-fledged development.

Early Egypt

The first evidence of a middle class in the history of man was in the Old Kingdom of Egypt (about 2980-2475 B.C.).[2] In this period the various arts and industries had developed to such a high state as to indicate middle class activity. But of this middle class we have practically no factual information. Its members kept their records on papyrus rolls, most of which have long since perished; and they left no monumental tombs, as did their illustrious rulers. The existence of a strong, centralized government provided the primary requirement for middle class development. But the second requirement—tolerant secular and religious authority which would permit rational thought on a broad scale—was lacking. The

---

[1] James Henry Breasted, *Ancient Times: A History of the Early World* (Boston: Ginn and Company, 1914), pp. 186-188. It was not the middle class in this instance which overcame transportation problems, but it is nevertheless a case in point.

[2] Breasted, *A History of Egypt*, p. 85. See also G. Steindorff and K. C. Seele, *When Egypt Ruled the East* (Chicago: The University of Chicago Press, 1942), pp. 11-23 and J. A. Wilson, *The Burden of Egypt* (Chicago: The University of Chicago Press, 1951), pp. 43-103.

construction of the Great Pyramids for the self-aggrandizement and supposed immortality of the monarchs was hardly an indication of a rational mental climate. Moreover, the predominantly agricultural basis of the Egyptian society, which is manifest at all periods of its history, precluded a very high development of trade and commerce. In the Middle Kingdom (2160-1788 B.C.) a more advanced type of economy became possible. This was the age of Egyptian feudalism, in which trade and plundering campaigns extended intercourse as far as Syria to the north, Crete to the northwest, and the Punt on the southern coast of the Red Sea. The economic infiltration process was underway. It led eventually to the expansion of the Egyptian state into imperial proportions (1580-1150 B.C.). At this point, however, the limit of expansion, absorption, followed by further expansion, was reached. Local loyalties within the imperial areas proved to be too strong for the broader loyalties which were necessary if the expanded unit was to develop a strong cohesive force. The crisis which took place centered around the religious controversy aroused by the visionary Pharaoh, Ikhnaton, who ruled in the fourteenth century before Christ. His advanced concept of a single universal God, Aton, would have provided the necessary cohesive religious conveyance for cultural unification of the larger political unit, but the concept was much too elevated for a people whose cultural training had not attained such an advanced degree of abstraction. The local and vested interests of the Amon priesthood predominated. In the political sphere also the needed organizational conveyances were lacking. Moreover, the system of transportation was slow, cumbersome, and uncertain. The insidious expansive influences of trade and commerce and the growing opulence and pervasive activities of the incipient middle class whom we can just glimpse now and again in the historical records had proven sufficient to bring about the imperial expansion of Egypt. But in the absence of supporting conveyances which would have cemented this larger organization into a unified state of comparative magnitude, the expansive movement was checked, and the larger organization eventually collapsed under the pressure of the Bedouins and the Hittites to the north and east and the Libyans to the west.

In the period of decadence (1150-525 B.C.) the decline of middle class activity is traced in successive waves or stages until the once powerful Egyptian supremacy reaches pitiful levels. But this last period marks the rise of middle class activity in other areas, notably Greece, which will be traced separately. It is noteworthy, however, to see how, as early as 1100 B.C., the collapse of Egyptian supremacy had caused a similar decline in trade. We have the pathetic story of the Egyptian envoy who was sent by Ramses XII to Byblos in Lebanon to purchase cedar for his Pharaoh.[3] The envoy—Wenamon, by name—was given an entirely inadequate sum of silver with which to pay for the cedar, and therefore carried also an image of Amon called "Amon-of-the-Way," as a gift to the prince of Byblos, in the hope that it might provide sufficient additional recompense. Wenamon was forced to carry letters to pass through the Egyptian Delta, by this time in foreign hands, and to travel on a Syrian ship. En route he was robbed of his silver, but managed by adroit action which bordered on thievery to replace it. Arriving at Byblos, he was at first refused an audience by the prince, Zakar-Baal, and was ordered to leave the city. Finally, through the intervention of a powerful religious fanatic in the court of the prince, he did manage to obtain an audience. The account of this audience provides us with a remarkably clear picture of the depths to which Egyptian prestige had fallen. Zakar-Baal in a long harangue acknowledges the cultural debt which he and his people owe to Egypt, but he disclaims all political obligations, and insists upon payment in full for the proposed purchase. The further adventures of the astute Wenamon, who labored under such difficulties, make interesting reading, but they need not concern us here.

The period of the supremacy of Egypt had been inextricably bound up with the activities of her middle class. Through the

[3] Breasted, *A History of Egypt*, pp. 513-518.

pervasive activities of this class she expanded and became great. But when fundamental conveyances failed in the larger arena the newborn civilization failed, and we must look elsewhere for further development. Henceforth Egypt was to become an insignificant agricultural portion of a greater society. Her middle class, unable any longer to engage in productive activity, simply faded out.

Mesopotamia

The center of gravity in the ancient world shifts from Northern Africa to Western Asia—the valleys of the Tigris and Euphrates, and Syria, or what is known as the Fertile Crescent, which sweeps north and west from the Persian Gulf until it turns south again along the shores of the eastern Mediterranean. The earliest records, which appear to begin about 3200 B.C., reveal a class of free, landholding citizens, rich in slaves, who engaged in extensive caravan and river trade.[4] Over them were the priests and government officials of the city-state. There was no national government; the gods were local deities; the city ruler was concerned only with two things, maintenance of the canals and dikes, and warfare with neighboring city-states. Already we can see the pervasive influence of the middle class as it reaches out its fingers of trade, and thereby creates a common language, a broadening horizon, and an increasing economic dependence upon the resources of outside areas—all of them influences which will lead on to political and religious expansion.

The first unification was under Sargon. It resulted ultimately in the Kingdom of Sumer and Akkad under the leadership of the city-state Ur. It lasted from 2418 to 2067 B.C., and it was during this period that the foundations of commercialism were laid. The middle class became a definite and important part of the society. In 2067-2025 B.C., under the leadership of its king Hammurabi, Babylon assumed the leading position. A system of law and order,

[4] Breasted, *The Conquest of Civilization*, Chap. IV.

such as had never existed before, now pervaded the dual valley. The growing middle class bloomed in the congenial atmosphere. The first step in the expanding and consolidating process had been successful. Through their pervasive influence the middle classes of the various city-states had brought about an imperialism which had now resulted in a larger state, fully unified through the adequate support of other conveyances. The powerful middle class in this larger state was now ready to continue its insidious activities on a yet grander scale. The king of Babylon represented the unified secular authority, while the Babylonian deities, Marduk and Ishtar, became the leading deities in the new state.

But one essential conveyance was lacking. Egypt, surrounded by complete desert, had enjoyed a degree of isolation which permitted uninterrupted internal development. The people of the Fertile Crescent had an entirely different problem. The semi-arid plains and hills on their borders were extremely fertile in the production of hardy, warlike hordes who pressed in periodically upon the settled areas. These periodic invasions—the Akkadians were originally invaders of this sort—stimulated change and ultimate progress, but they also temporarily interrupted the middle class development at frequent intervals. Such was the fate of the Babylonian middle class. It had barely started its catalytic work when the Kassites swept in from the hills, and the Babylonian progress in civilization was arrested for nearly a thousand years. Nevertheless, the Syrian culture on the borders of the Mediterranean continued. The energetic Aramean[5] middle class extended its business activities far beyond its own political borders until Aramean commerce permeated all of Western Asia. Like the Jews in modern times, the Arameans were not bound into a political union but they were the trading people of the period. Through their influence Aramean became the universal language of the age. The intercommunication which they encouraged laid the foundation for a larger and more stable political union of the people of the Fertile Crescent.

[5] The Syrians were frequently called Arameans.

The Assyrians (750-612 B.C.) established the first of these unions. The extreme emphasis they laid upon militarism proved to be their weakness. The Assyrians were militarily strong enough to seize control by force, but they lacked the ability to develop or assimilate other conveyances to hold their conquests. After a brief interregnum during which the Chaldean Empire flourished, the old rulers quickly gave way to the advancing Medes and Persians.

The Persian Empire (530-330 B.C.) marked the greatest advance of the Oriental middle class. The culture developed was now rapidly being transferred to the Mediterranean world, where the Greeks were ready to receive it. Under Persian rule a strong centralized government, secular and religious toleration, freedom from warfare at home, an adequate monetary system, and a good transportation system all existed. But there was now a sixth factor which acted as a restraint on further development. All the Oriental governments were characteristically despotic. They were nominally a system of rule by one man, although they usually operated as a bureaucracy.[6] Under such conditions middle class development could never proceed beyond a certain point. For further progress we must cast our eyes westward to Europe, where the democratic spirit was a force, and consequently where the spirit of individualism, so necessary a part of middle class development, was operative under more favorable conditions.

[6] V. Gordon Childe develops at length the argument that the river-valley dwellers of Egypt, Mesopotamia, and India were so economically dependent upon bureaucratic controls over irrigation and other matters that an individualistic spirit could not exist. See his book, *Man Makes Himself*, pp. 104-112.

CHAPTER FOUR

The First Industrial Revolution

Societal Phases

Perhaps the basic reason that history appears to proceed in great cycles upon occasion, although always in a variable form, is that each new civilization retraces old steps which its predecessors have already covered. Thus, a civilization may proceed so far in its development before its conveyances fail and the broader loyalties break down under the pressure of the local loyalties. The successor civilization, which is ordinarily made up of more primitive peoples, then picks up, not where the older civilization left off, but at a much earlier stage. It painfully and slowly works its way up to the previous level, and if its conveyances are superior, proceeds to new levels before eventually collapsing. Such temporary reversion is by no means inevitable, as we shall note when we come to the American culture, but it has occurred frequently enough to permit us to see certain characteristic phases. These phases are, broadly, (1) a primitive, communal mode of life already described; (2) the emergence of a barbaric ruler-slave state wherein the rule of force predominates; (3) a feudalistic state in which we begin to perceive an incipient middle class development; (4) renewed emphasis upon centralized authority and the promotion of broader loyalties under tyranny; (5) the eventual triumph of a more or less fully fledged middle class which, if really successful, leads the society on to capitalism and economic imperialism, and (6) a partial expansion of the middle class to include some of the proletariat.

Thus far civilizations have developed at one time or another. What phases may lie beyond only future events can show. The last phase mentioned is not a stable one, although it is certainly of a static nature in comparison with the highly dynamic fifth phase. It encourages special privileges and monopolies, which restrict further action of the individualist. Initiative is submerged in adherence to precedence. Three factors help to bring about the reversion to staticism. First, the successful members of the middle class gain privileged positions, and move into the ruling class. They learn to operate as a team in which certain rules are observed as a matter of course. These rules, which may be either subversive, such as trusts or cartels, or ethical, such as business codes which these successful business leaders build up, hamper the free play of competitive forces and individual initiative.

At the other end of the social hierarchy the proletariat or laboring groups learn to act collectively for mutual advantage. They are not shrewd enough or outstanding enough in ability to prosper through individual action, so they learn to work collectively in order to gain privileges. Both the business leaders and the proletariat use state authority wherever possible to legalize their privileges. Regardless of which group gains the upper hand in the maneuvers for political domination—that is, regardless of whether the state moves toward socialism or toward fascism—the true middle class individualist is caught in the tangle of the tightening restrictions. The dynamic elements which he had fostered through his catalytic activity gradually disappear, and the society slowly lapses into staticism.

True, now and again an outstanding middle class individualist will emerge who will reactivate for a time the dynamic elements in the society. Such individualists will refuse to abide by the rules set up by the privileged groups and, through their decisive actions, will force a revision of such rules whereby progressive action is fostered once more. But as the institutional factors become more and more rigid, and as the conveyances are subjected to greater and greater strain, these flare-ups in progressive activity become increasingly rare. The society turns gradually from material considerations, and in its maturity evolves a deepening interest in aesthetic ideals. Meanwhile the now completely monopolistic and restrictive actions of the vested interests undermine the broader loyalties and so bring about the ultimate collapse of the civilization.

Here again the process is not even, but rather convulsive. Outstanding military leaders will be able to resurrect something of the old broader loyalties from time to time, and will bring about a temporary restoration, but such resurrections do not reactivate the middle class individualists, for military rule is almost completely restrictive; therefore these flashes of apparent revitalization become more rare until they cease. This gradual breakdown period is well described by Toynbee in his period of universality, which then merges into a series of "rallies and routs" until the whole structure finally collapses.

The six stages in the course of a civilization will be considered again later in much greater detail. Meanwhile it will be of interest to examine some of the principal features of the Greek civilization which was now emerging in and around the Aegean Sea.

Early Greece

During the period 2000-1000 B.C. the Greek invaders from the north slowly displaced the Minoan civilization which had had its center at Crete.[1] Too little is known of this action for us to appreciate the significant details, but it is evident that the displacement was fairly well completed by about 1200-1100 B.C. The Greeks were meanwhile making the transition from a nomadic way of life to a settled existence. They passed through the second

[1] Breasted, *The Conquest of Civilization*, Chap. IX.

stage of kings and formation of class structure fairly rapidly, so that by 1000-750 B.C. the feudalistic stage of development had been reached. The rapidity with which these first steps were covered may have been due partly to the extensive cultural influence of the older Oriental civilizations, for the Greeks borrowed freely from the old Minoan civilization, from Egypt, and from the civilizations of the Fertile Crescent. But the independent spirit of these barbaric invaders was also a factor. In any case, while class structure and stratification did occur, the size of the upper classes in proportion to the lower was much greater than in any of the earlier civilizations. The ruler-slave stage which we can just glimpse in the records bore little relation to the ruler-slave stages of the Oriental civilizations. Slavery did become and remained a distinct part of Greek culture, but a relatively large proportion of the population continued to be free.

The other peculiar feature of Greek development was the emphasis upon segmentation of state authority into city-states. Although the transportation and communication facilities were good enough to assure a common language, a common religion, and a common culture, the decentralizing influences in the form of geographical setting and independent spirit were great enough to prevent a complete coagulation into a single state. This continued decentralization of state authority encouraged individual initiative and thereby proved advantageous to the budding middle class, but it was also instrumental in bringing about the eventual collapse of the Greek civilization. In the crucial later stages the broader loyalties failed, and left the individualistic city-states open to foreign conquest.

By 650 B.C. the fourth stage of development had begun.[2] Tyrants arose in the various cities as champions of the lower classes. By this means the power of the nobles was restrained, special and restrictive privileges which the nobles had built up were partially broken down, and the way was thereby opened for the enterprising middle class individualists to begin their pervasive

[2] *Ibid.*, Chap. XII.

and dynamic work on a full scale. This fourth stage, that of re-newed emphasis upon centralization, accompanied by a partial breakdown and rearrangement of the class structure, is always a critical period in any civilization. If it is not largely successful the feudalistic rigidities are not properly removed, and the subse-quent middle class emergence may be largely abortive. In that case the civilization moves toward universality and ultimate decay before it has attained a very high level of culture. On the other hand, the centralization process may easily proceed too far. The unifying force in the form of tyrants or absolute monarchies then becomes too restrictive and as a result the necessary degree of tol-eration for full middle class development is lacking. It is notable that the Greeks passed through this stage with a high degree of success. Through the tyrants the special privileges of the nobles were sufficiently broken down to permit middle class infiltration, but the tyrants themselves were not permitted to gain such ab-solute authority as to endanger individualism. The Greek civiliza-tion was now ready to move on to the fifth stage, that of capital-ism and economic imperialism.

Uses of Wealth

This brings us to a distinction which is fundamental for a proper appreciation of capitalistic growth. Wealth may be used for im-mediate consumption. But such wealth is not capital. Capital is wealth which is used to buy something other than immediate consumption. If the wealth is stored for later consumption, such as the storing of grain in Egypt by Joseph for the anticipated seven lean years, the accumulated wealth merely provides for fu-ture consumption without any addition to the stock of wealth itself. Such use of wealth is the first stage removed from immedi-ate consumption. It allows for periodic rather than continual pro-duction, and thereby introduces a greater degree of flexibility into societal life. The next stage is reached when a stock of capital is used to buy power or status. The simplest illustration of this use is the manufacture of arms for conquest. If the conquest is successful, and that is the risk taken, the conqueror gains a return on his investment by exploiting the conquered. Actually such use of capital is productive, since the improved societal organization, as in Egypt, results in greater output. Yet the prime purpose is to facilitate the transfer of future production from one class to another. The third use of capital begins when wealth is produced for exchange rather than for consumption. This introduces the middleman or trader. Nominally the exchange of wealth merely adds to subjective utility or satisfactions by bringing into the hands of the consumer items for consumption in a variety or pattern which pleases him most. But the actual effect of such exchange is much more far-reaching. It permits specialization and a division of labor which results in greater productive efficiency. This increased efficiency is sufficient not only to maintain the new trading class, but also to provide a greater volume of production for other classes in the society. Merchant capital is therefore exceedingly productive.

This brings us to the distinction between commercial capital and industrial capital. Commercial capital is that which is used to facilitate the transfer of wealth among individuals through exchange. The merchant is interested solely in buying commodities from various sources and in selling these commodities in other markets at an advanced price. In developing his sources and his markets he is primarily aggressive, competitive, and individualistic. But once he has his markets developed his viewpoint alters. In his purchases he seeks to gain a monopsonistic advantage, while in his sales he seeks to establish a monopolistic position. Although merchant capitalists may be progressive and individualistic in the earlier stages of trading development, they soon cease to work toward an extension of the market and begin to concentrate upon exploitation of the given market. Their viewpoint is then restrictive; they now have a privileged position which they wish to defend.

Industrial capital is somewhat different. It is capital which is used in the actual production process in order to improve productive efficiency. Insofar as the industrial capitalist is successful he gets an ever-increasing flow of production for which he must find a market. Since the best way to lower his costs is to improve techniques and to use more industrial capital in the production process, he is progressive in that direction. Also, since the mass production system necessitates ever-expanding markets, he is equally aggressive in that direction. As a consequence, the industrial capitalist continues to be individualistic and progressive long after the merchant capitalist has become restrictive.

There is a limit, of course, to the expansive and dynamic influence exerted by the industrial capitalist just as there was for the merchant capitalist. When the industrial capitalist begins to reach the outer limits of markets in which he can sell, he, too, begins to view the possibilities of privilege with favor. Instead of extending the market further, either extensively or intensively, it becomes easier to press down labor costs. In this way costs are lowered without causing an embarrassing increase in production. If the industrial capitalist has been expanding his market intensively, the downward pressure on labor costs will affect the ability of the labor class to purchase the product; but since the Greeks relied upon slave labor which did not at any time share appreciably in the increased production, that factor did not enter into the problem.

Greek Industry

The Phoenicians had earlier moved into the field of industrial capitalism on a limited scale, but it was the Greeks who really developed industrial production on a mass production basis for the first time. Pottery factories, extensive smithies for metalwork, and even cloth manufacture on an extensive scale grew up in Athens and other Greek centers. The actual progress of this early industrial revolution is difficult to trace. Beyond broad, generalizing statements the economic influences of early Greek civilization are lost in obscurity.

Because of the lack of factual information we cannot be sure of how much the various influences operated to bring the Greek industrial age to an end. The failure of the Hellenic states to unite effectively into a cohesive nation is well known and it was undoubtedly the fundamental reason for the ultimate collapse of Greek sovereignty. The loose union of the Greek city-states was sufficient to withstand the Oriental despotism of Persia. Indeed, under the leadership of their Macedonian conquerors the Greeks were able to spread the Hellenistic culture throughout the Near East. But when they were pitted against the powerful and cohesive military might of the Romans the lack of unity among the Greek states became most apparent. Rome through her adroit diplomacy was able to foster this disunity until at last the Greek world came piecemeal under Roman political authority. Thereafter the Hellenic states continued only as a series of Roman provinces, each exploited by the common overlord without regard to commercial development.

The other factors more difficult to discern were the gradual development of monopolistic rigidities as merchant capitalists and, later, industrial capitalists, sought to assure privileged positions, the debasement of the coinage system, and the increasing number of state restrictions which gradually evolved as more and more emphasis came to be placed upon military strength. The restriction of middle class development to free citizens limited the extent to which capitalism could expand. Yet the fact that the eastern part of the Roman Empire continued to be the more progressive commercially would indicate that commercial monopoly was not as restrictive a factor as the political coercion. Also, it is notable that the debasement of the coinage proceeded at a much more rapid pace in Rome itself and in the western provinces than it did in the eastern provinces.[3] It was not until about A.D.

[3] Elgin Groseclose, *Money: The Human Conflict* (Norman: University of Oklahoma Press, 1934), Bk. III.

1100 that coinage debasement became a fundamental influence in the disintegration of the Byzantine Empire. The very fact that the Byzantine Empire outlasted its western partner by over a thousand years attests to the virility of the Greek industrialism which had been built up.[4]

The actual growth and decline of the Roman Empire itself do not provide good illustrative material for tracing the growth of the middle class. In the political sphere Rome contributed greatly to the European civilization, but commercially her contributions were for the most part negative. She used her political domination as a means for material exploitation of the provinces, and as a result her form of capitalism was almost entirely of the third type outlined earlier in the chapter, namely, the use of wealth for systematic conquest and exploitation. Through her restrictive and coercive political actions she hampered and probably halted the further development of the Greek industrialization process. It might be said that the continued commercial and industrial activity in the eastern Mediterranean proceeded in spite of rather than because of Roman authority.

Our attention is now diverted to the new civilization which was beginning to arise in Europe. By tracing the successive stages in its growth it will be possible to get a more complete picture of some of the basic factors underlying our own culture.

[4] *Ibid.*, p. 33.

CHAPTER FIVE

Prelude to the Second Industrial Revolution

Early Medieval Period

Under Rome the Greek culture, cast into Latin form, reached its utmost limits. The internal development of the culture had reached its climax before the Roman military expansion exerted its influence on the Hellenistic world. Thereafter the process was one of Latinization and geographical dispersion. Just as the Egyptian culture continued to exert a broad influence long after the internal development had ceased, so the Greco-Roman culture continued to spread through the European area long after Rome had ceased to exert her military and political authority. After the fall of Rome the authority was purely mental and emotional, that is, religious. In the Middle Ages the unifying concept of a universal Christian church served to bind the primitive Germanic peoples into a loose cultural unit in which the common Germanic dialects were fused even further by the influence of the universal Latin tongue. Latin became the classic language which all the tribes used and from which they all borrowed freely to form vulgarized or so-called Romance or semi-Romance tongues.

This acculturation process greatly speeded up the movement from the primitive stage, through the ruler-slave stage, and to the feudalistic era. As a result a rigid system of slavery did not have an opportunity to crystallize before the feudalistic pattern had evolved. As a consequence class distinctions, though rigorous enough, were not drawn so sharply as to destroy utterly the comparative social freedoms which had existed in the primitive communal society. Members of the lowest class became serfs and villeins but not slaves. As a result, the breaking down of class rigidities by the new incipient middle class, which began to emerge almost immediately, proceeded much more rapidly than it had in the Oriental civilizations, and somewhat more rapidly even than it had proceeded in the early Greek society. By borrowing culture as it did in the period from A.D. 500 to 1000 the new European culture was able to move quickly through the earlier stages of its growth and therefore had a better opportunity to evolve to a higher plane while institutional factors were still fluid. Moreover, by borrowing useful conveyances instead of having to build them up the European culture was able to avoid many of the rigidities and vestigial encumbrances which such a building-up process would have entailed.

By A.D. 1000 the European culture had definitely reached the feudalistic stage wherein the absolute power of the kings was being restrained by a fairly numerous nobility. In this reasonably favorable climate where there was a fair amount of law and order, coupled with some measure of toleration so that nonbelligerent shrewdness could flourish, the new middle class was able to begin once again to exert its insidious and pervasive influence on the society.

Hypothetical Group

To appreciate just what does occur in the growth of a civilization a purely hypothetical illustration may be used. Suppose there were ten groups with ten people in each group, and suppose further that primitive communal life broke down as soon as more than ten people formed a single unit. This illustration entails merely a reduction in numbers from the real situation in order to show the subjective forces at work more clearly. In the groups of ten the leader was not sufficiently separated from his followers to adopt a purely exploitive viewpoint. Consequently the family and associational affections were sufficiently strong to prevent a distinct caste system from developing. The chieftain and the weakling in the group were still on somewhat similar planes. But as soon as the primitive groupings were merged into the larger unit of one hundred persons, family and associational affections were too restrictive to encompass the group. The narrow family loyalties, or local loyalties, as we have named them, continued as cohesive elements within the entire group; but because they were pitted against each other the evolution of a broader loyalty was needed in order to hold the group of one hundred together. This was accomplished by one means only, namely, physical force. Of the various chieftains one inevitably emerged victorious over the others. But, as Machiavelli points out, it is one thing to get power and quite another to keep it. The new leader used his trusted associates within his own group to maintain authority, but also, in order to restrain them and to build up interests of other groups in the new broader loyalty he had established, the new leader, now a king, brought in wherever possible leading members of the unrepresented groups. If a leader of one of these groups was intractable, he had to be exterminated. This one group, then, without representation in the new authority was very likely to gravitate to the lowest social level. The various groups of ten thus were shuffled into position in such a manner that the king with a few military followers of varying importance exerted absolute control over the remaining members of the enlarged group. Seven or eight under the leadership of one were the rulers over the ninety odd.

To insure his control even further the king used religious authority to gain domination over the minds of all members of the new group. The local deities became fused in a new national religion. The religious authority thus formed was normally vested in the king. He assumed godlike attributes in the minds of his subjects. The religious authority necessitated the formation of a priestly class in which the chief priest or priests became highly significant members of the newly created nobility. They might even exert a power parallel to that of the king himself, but being oligarchical rather than monarchical in development and relying upon mental rather than physical control, the religious authority was ordinarily subject to the power of the king. The universal religion of the group of one hundred now reinforced the unified political authority. Two broader loyalties had now been built up as cohesive factors.

But the unity was one of fear, whereby the few dominated the many through physical force, ultimately sanctioned by state regulation and religious coercion in the form of the church. Moreover, the ruling class itself was subject to the absolute power of the monarch. The system was purely exploitive from the top down.

With the lowly followers well at heel, the next step was the struggle for power among the members of the ruling class. Several forces acted to weaken the despotic control of the monarch over his immediate followers. First, in the lineal descent immature or incapable rulers invariably inherited the throne from time to time. Such occasions gave the more powerful nobles an opportunity to gain extra privileges in the state and more control over their individual domains. Sometimes one of them might usurp the throne, and thus begin a new dynasty; but the dispersion of power continued, regardless of such upsets.

Second, royal descendants formed an upper nobility with extraordinary rights and privileges, thus rivaling the power of their ruler kinsman. Third, with the growth of the state in population and geographic extent many authorities usually exercised by the king alone had to be deputized. The noble deputies became in this way small monarchs in their own right. These and other causes operated to weaken the centralized control of the king. The nobles gradually came to form a feudalistic system of control.

Growth of Commerce

Such was the stage reached in the various parts of Europe in the early medieval period. With the feudalistic era, the more enterprising but nonbelligerent members of the lower class were able to begin their individualistic activities on a broad scale. In Europe we find such individuals forming trading centers, particularly at points where people could congregate easily to exchange goods and services. Coastal and river towns sprang up throughout the whole area, but it is significant that the Western European countries, where intercommunication encouraged a progressive spirit, developed more rapidly in this respect than Eastern European countries. These towns in the beginning were under the direct control of the local lord. The townsmen probably gained their freedom from thralldom originally by buying it with wealth gained through shrewd manipulations, as mentioned earlier. Now these middle class townsmen frequently used the same tactics in gaining privileges and various freedoms for the town. In return for a lump sum payment a charter might be purchased, supposedly good in perpetuity. The noble selling the charter ordinarily wanted the funds to wage a private war against a rival noble, or to go on a crusade, so that the actual payment very likely ended back in the coffers of the townsmen in return for goods and services the noble required for his military equipage. These towns soon became the meccas for the more enterprising serfs and villeins who escaped by one means or another from their lord's estate. In this way the middle class obtained a continuous new supply of enterprising members who were ready to pick up and carry on the tradition of individual initiative where the more established and more prosperous townsmen left off as they moved into privileged positions.

But as the institutional rigidities and special privileges of established middleclass townsmen multiplied, the new guild system stifled further development. The Crusades had opened up trade with the Near East and indirectly with the Far East; but even this expansion was insufficient to bring about more than an incipient development of the new middle class. By A.D. 1400 the extremely high middleman rates being charged by the Italian city-states for goods from the East and the rigid guild regulations which had grown up in all of the Western European towns attested to the powerful influence of mercantile capital. Thus far the middle class had come, but now in the absence of other favorable influences its further growth and development would have been partially arrested, and the higher stages of civilization might never have been reached before the society moved onward into the phases of universality and ultimate decline.

European Expansion

But just at this critical stage three distinct and simultaneous occurrences operated to change the entire picture. First, the feuding barons in their struggles with one another became so few in number and so impoverished that it was relatively easy for the tyrant kings to establish themselves. Thus we see the decline of the nobles and the rise of the tyrants in Austria, Spain, Portugal, France, the Netherlands, and England. Italy and Germany failed to go through this phase until later, so that even though the other occurrences affected them, a complete middle class development was arrested for the time being. Russia, of course, was still a ruler-slave state.

At the same time as these tyrant kings were rising in Western European countries and thereby broadening the basis for middle class activity, the Turks moved into the Eastern Mediterranean area. As a result of the Turkish advance two new factors were introduced. First, the trade route to the Far East was cut off. Second, the Byzantine scholars of Constantinople were driven westward to Italy. The cutting off of the Mediterranean route to the Far East compelled the Western European countries to look elsewhere for a trade route to the Orient. The extremely high middleman rates charged by the Italian city-states had irked the Western countries, so that the search for an alternative route resulted from a double motivation. Just how much influence the Byzantine scholars exerted upon the westward expansion is difficult to ascertain. The period from 1453 until the first voyage of Columbus in 1492 is so brief that the new spirit of inquiry and enterprise which the Byzantine scholars infused into the European arena could hardly have gained much force. It is significant, however, that Columbus brought his daring ideas from Italy, where the renascent spirit was beginning to flourish, and applied them to the needs of Spain. John Cabot likewise brought his advanced ideas to England.

The Middle Class Spirit in Flower

However much the new ideas of the budding Renaissance may have influenced the original westward expansion, or however much the double motivation may have brought about a spontaneous exploratory movement, there is no question about the repercussions of the new discoveries upon the European civilization. Men's minds were stirred; a progressive spirit was instilled in the society which made it easier for the Humanist movement to gain a foothold. The thrilling revelation of an unknown and highly promising Eldorado in the west turned men's thoughts away from the inbound and repetitious concentration upon spiritual factors, which the universal church emphasized, to the material considerations of this world. Men felt a new power surging within themselves, experienced a new sense of mastery over their physical environment. It was a mental climate of challenge, of assurance, of excitement, and of change. Into this favorable climate the practical and scientific thoughts of the Greek philosophers were infused. Men turned eagerly to the ancients for guidance in the new situation. They rediscovered the free and dynamic spirit of scientific inquiry which the ethical postulates of Augustine and later of Thomas Aquinas had sought to restrain. In such an at-

mosphere individualistic and materialistic middle class activity
flourished. The growth and development of this class, which had
been momentarily arrested by the crystallization of the guild
system, now proceeded more rapidly than ever. Restrictive privileges and institutional elements were swept away one by one and
the fluidity of social forms so necessary for social change was restored.

The first and most important victory of the middle class was
the breaking down of the universal church.[1] Clearly abusive prac-
tices, such as the wholesale distribution of indulgences and par-
dons, could not for a moment withstand the searching scrutiny of
even the most elementary forms of scientific thought. In Italy
the lack of unity prevented a concerted attack on the church
from gaining headway, but in Germany the powerful Nordic
spirit of individualism which had never died out was enough to
overcome this weakness. The northern principalities took up
the cause of Luther in a manner which he had not anticipated,
and forced the issue to the point where a complete rupture was
effected. The other northern states quickly followed the example
of Germany, and the Protestant movement became widespread.

The division between the north and the south on religious
postulates led to a great struggle for control over border areas.
The old universal church, which we can now call in its more restricted sense the Roman Catholic Church, fought desperately to
hold its ground. In Italy and in Spain the weakness of the middle
class quickly settled the issue, but the struggle was more unde-
cided in England and in France. England vacillated back and forth
in the first half of the sixteenth century until the political struggle with Spain for control of the Atlantic swung the English
definitely into the Protestant stronghold. In France, the issue was
even more closely drawn, and for a time it appeared as though
she too would become Protestant. The forces of reaction even-

---

[1] In a materialistic study of this sort the services rendered by the universal
church in carrying and spreading the culture of earlier civilizations cannot be
properly recognized and evaluated.

tually won out, partly because the middle class development was less advanced, particularly in the south, and partly because of the chronic rivalry with the English. But in the struggle the results were less conclusive than they had been in Spain or in Italy. Moreover, the Roman Catholic Church had been compelled to improve its moral standards, to reorganize itself on a more liberal basis, and to formulate a more tolerant policy toward its members. In France and in other northern areas Roman Catholicism came to have an entirely different meaning from its meaning in the more reactionary countries of the Mediterranean. As a result middle class individualism came to be tolerated within the formal structure of the Roman Catholic Church wherever such individualism was strong enough to insist upon such toleration.

Within the Protestant group, and also within the more progressive Roman Catholic groups to a lesser extent, a new ethical code was formulated. Max Weber and R. H. Tawney argue that this ethical code led to the middle class development and the second industrial revolution.[2] When the broader viewpoint is taken, however, as has been attempted in this study, it appears more likely that the resurgent middle class unconsciously formulated an ethical code which suited its desires. This middle class wished to push religion out of the mundane world wherever possible, and thus allow free and individualistic activity to proceed in the more favorable atmosphere of secular inquiry. Ethical considerations were still a potent force even in the secular arena, but they were reformulated to suit the middle class viewpoint. The habit of industriousness became a sign of virtue, whereas formerly it had been a sign of servility. The ruling class, because of its general emphasis upon exploitation rather than upon creativeness and industry, had looked always upon the producer as a low class person bearing the taint of a slave. The new middle class, however, emphasized the honor of labor; the producer now became the person

[2] Max Weber, *The Protestant Ethic and the Spirit of Capitalism* (New York: Charles Scribner's Sons, 1930); and R. H. Tawney, *The Acquisitive Society* (New York: Harcourt, Brace & Company, 1920).

to be esteemed, while the dilettante was a person to be despised much as one would despise any parasite.

The second great virtue of the Protestant ethic which the middle class formulated was that of thrift. Probably this virtue grew up partly as a result of habit, partly as an antithesis to the wasteful expenditures of the upper class, and partly as a means whereby the middle class individualist could further his creative activities.

The third factor was not so much a virtue in itself as a result of the first two virtues, and of the individual initiative of the members of the new middle class. Being industrious, these middle class individuals produced in substantial quantities; being thrifty, they did not consume as rapidly as they produced. Since each middle class individualist was intensely interested in materialistic advancement and since he worked and thought in a secular atmosphere of scientific inquiry and progressiveness, an extensive use of accumulated wealth for the production of new wealth was a natural and inevitable development. A second era of industrial capitalism soon got underway.

The first struggle of the industrial capitalists was with the upper stratum within the middle class. This upper stratum, which was composed largely of mercantile capitalists, had developed the third use of capital whereby a geographic division of labor was made possible through trade and commerce. It had then built up a tradition of privilege and monopoly which the new industrial capitalists had to break down in order to proceed with their expanding system of intensive division of labor. The second struggle was with the guild members or craftsmen. Therefore it is possible to discern at this period (A.D. 1500-1700) seven different groups within the society, each trying to obtain or maintain a favorable position in the rapidly changing social order. There were the medieval rulers still nominally in power, the Roman Catholic Church struggling with the new Protestant movement, the mercantile capitalists anxious to maintain their trading privileges, and the guild craftsmen also with privileges to defend. Arrayed against these reactionary forces were the new industrial capitalists and the serfs who were now rapidly obtaining their freedom. The last group was numerically large but socially impotent. The industrial capitalists, on the other hand, though numerically few in number, were the most important group of all, for they carried the force of individualism and initiative. Moreover, to assist them in the struggle, they had the Protestant movement, the spreading influence of scientific thought brought on by the Renaissance, and the physical impact of a vast new frontier to the west.

CHAPTER SIX

The Second Industrial Revolution: I

Relative Positions of Western European Countries

The broad courses of future development were drawn. It now remained to be seen in which part of the European culture the industrial revolution would take place first. Italy, with a strong orthodox religious background, an underdeveloped middle class, and a firmly entrenched mercantilist viewpoint, served only as a door whereby the ancient culture of the classical civilization was passed to the rest of Europe. Germany had the individualistic middle class spirit but lacked two essential conveyances for a successful industrial revolution at this time. First, she had not yet been united by tyrant kings, and, second, she lacked an adequate means of transportation and communication. The Rhine was not sufficient for this purpose. Because of Germany's slower development the upper class had time to gain an important lead in the struggle for position in the new order. Consequently the industrial development when it did come was paternalistic in form. The new individualism was permitted only limited scope, and the state continued to be all-powerful.

The other five areas for potential industrial development were Spain, Portugal, France, the Netherlands, and England. Spain had a good system of transportation and it was first in the field of westward expansion. Yet, after a brief period of glory and leadership, it faded out. The basic reason, of course, was the lack of a middle class in Spain. There the Roman Catholic tradition was strong, and heretical and individualistic tendencies of the incipient middle class were not tolerated. The Inquisition prevented any really new thinking from flourishing within the Iberian Peninsula. The Portuguese government was somewhat more tolerant in this respect, and some middle class development in this period is discernible. Yet Portugal lacked certain essential conveyances for an early industrial revolution. State and religious toleration were not complete. On the other hand, Portugal, through her expansion south and eastward, did manage to infuse a more liberal spirit into the home traditions. Probably the real limiting factor in the Portuguese development was lack of freedom from warfare in the home area. Portugal was restricted and limited at all times by the neighboring might of Spain.

France came much nearer to assuming the mantle of leadership in this next great and momentous stage in the Western European culture. For centuries France had led England in cultural development. But now at this critical point she faltered in her leadership, and thereby lost her commanding position. The reasons for the French failure are numerous and difficult to assess. The religious struggle has already been mentioned, and certainly constitutes a primary reason. The movement of many middle class Huguenots to England and the colonies was a serious loss. But the basic reason really goes much deeper than that. In their struggle for control, the tyrant kings of France, beginning with Louis XI, were able to attain a dominant position without having to appeal to the lower classes within the society. The feudal system was therefore not destroyed as it was in England under the Tudor monarchs, but was perpetuated another three hundred years in an increasingly rigid form. The passage through the era of the tyrant kings was therefore not entirely successful. Middle class activity was restricted, though not altogether stifled as in Spain. Other factors of importance were lack of freedom from warfare in the home territory and slower means of transportation and communication in the inland areas.

Hypothetical Group Reconsidered

It might be of interest at this point to pick up our hypothetical group of one hundred persons where we left it in the last chapter. At this time it had just entered the feudalistic stage of development. This stage, which is partly a reversion to the earlier phase of disunity, is really quite temporary in spite of its seemingly static nature. It represents an attempt through institutionalism to stabilize the growth and change wrought by the creation of broader loyalties. It is in effect an era of retrenchment, when the society pauses, as it were, before proceeding to the next stage of complete integration into a compact and cohesive unit. No civilization which has proceeded as far as feudalism has ever failed to move on to the next stage of tyrant kings. But it is the manner and method of this development which determine how far the civilization will advance before it moves on eventually into the phase of universality and ultimate stagnation.

The movement of the ruler-slave society into feudalism marks an advance. Despotic control by one man over the enlarged and loosely integrated group gives way to oligarchical rule in which power is partly dispersed among the other eight or nine members of the ruling class. The attitude of this oligarchical group toward the ninety odd slave members is purely exploitive, but the dispersion of power offers a much greater opportunity for the more enterprising individualists within the slave group to improve their social status. An incipient middle class development now becomes discernible, and the slave group begins to differentiate generally. From a homogeneous mass we see the emergence of heterogeneous subgroups which commence to coagulate. At the top are the shrewd, nonbelligerent individualists who gain special privileges and status by personal initiative. At a lower level and in less clearly defined outline we begin to see the gradual formation of labor groups, special religious groups, small ethnical groups, sometimes intelligent but meek, sometimes simply stupid or un-cultured or both. These lower subgroups depend upon collective action for improvement of their status. The individualists within such groups may serve for a time as subgroup leaders, but soon desert and gravitate toward the middle class. At the feudalistic stage the middle class individualists have begun to assume a sig-nificant position in the society, while the lower continue to be largely undifferentiated.

Now comes the critical stage of tyrant kings. If the middle class development under feudalism was incomplete, then the ty-rant king phase will be for the most part an imperialistic despotism. The tyrant king will emerge as a champion of the lesser nobility only; while the middle class, lacking a champion, will fail to emerge as a full-fledged and powerful group within the society. Egypt is an example of this type of civilization. The ancient Egyptian society under the early Pharaohs never ceased to be a planned state under rigid secular and religious control. The middle class was unable to exert its dynamic influence to any great extent before the re-stricting elements of institutionalism took hold. The society moved from feudalism into an era of imperialistic greatness and then on into the phase of universality and ultimate decay with-out experiencing the eclectic development which a strong middle class could have brought about. An active middle class, through its emphasis upon individualism and initiative, breaks down local loyalties which exist in the form of ethnic groups, intolerant religious sects, privileged castes, or economic monopolies, and, through the development of superior conveyances, builds up the broader loyalties which are necessary for a high level of culture.

A second obstacle must also be overcome before a really suc-cessful middle class evolution becomes possible. The middle class may be sufficiently influential in the society to help the tyrant kings gain power, but if it lacks the power to force concessions from these monarchs once they do gain power, then the develop-ment is again abortive. The newly created tyrants may turn to the nobility, particularly the lesser nobility, and to the mercantile capitalists who have attained a position where they have privileges to protect and who are, therefore, no longer true individualists. On the basis of their support the tyrant kings may be able to restrain the individualistic tendencies of the true middle class, and thus may prevent further development in the society. The Greek middle class was able to prevent this restraint from occurring, but the French tyrant kings succeeded in restraining middle class growth for a time in that country. The French Revolution, when it did come, was distinctly a middle class revolt against a reactionary and decadent line of tyrant kings. But the delay permitted restrictions which were costly. The Huguenot middle class individualists had been driven out or restrained.

The Netherlands had an industrial revolution, and for a time the middle class activities in that area threatened to surpass those of the English. Many factors operated to encourage the emergence of the Dutch and Belgian middle class. Religious barriers were broken down in a successful Protestant movement. Transportation and communication facilities were exceedingly good. The government, after the overthrow of Spanish imperialism, was tolerant, and passed easily through the tyrant king period into democracy. But one factor was unfavorable, and that was the lack of freedom from warfare or fear of warfare in the home territory. Because it was part of the Continent the Netherlands did not have the freedom from European conflicts which was a vital factor in the English development.

Leadership of England

The English, therefore, pioneered in this next stage in the growth and development of the Western European civilization. Every one of the basic factors necessary for a full-fledged middle class emergence was favorable. The government conveyance was exceptionally good, since the powerful Tudor tyrants, after performing their task of unification, had been succeeded by the weak Stuarts, who were easily thrust aside and eventually replaced by a well-meaning and innocuous Hanoverian line. The religious conveyance was also excellently adapted to middle class development. The restrictive elements of the universal church had been swept away in the English Reformation, but the emergent church was not radical in form. The English thus had a strong central government and also a reasonable measure of democracy and religious toleration. The third favorable factor, as mentioned above, was freedom from war in the home area.

The fourth factor, an adequate but stable form of money, was very opportunely supplied at this time by Spain. The spectacular inflow of gold and silver to Spain from the New World came into the hands of the Spanish nobility. Though it helped Spain attain national glory for a brief period, the period of Spanish greatness was certain to be short-lived. The Spanish leaders did not have the military and organizational superiority which the Romans had possessed over their own contemporaries, and consequently, the purely exploitive use to which the Spaniards put the wealth did not yield a return. The precious metal flowed out of Spain as rapidly as it flowed in. It found its way into France, into the Netherlands, and in particular into England. The consumption goods which Spain received in return were soon used up, after which Spain lapsed gradually into insignificance. The Spaniards, like the medieval nobles who sold charters to middle class townsmen, gave up their power for a temporary satisfaction.

But the effect of this inflow of gold into the English economy was profound. It facilitated an expanding system of trade and commerce, an expansion which had previously been seriously hampered by an inadequate monetary conveyance. By 1600 the relative increase in gold and silver was again inadequate to accommodate the now rapidly growing production. Throughout the seventeenth century the English suffered chronically from monetary shortage. Recourse was made to credit facilities in the

Continent many times, until finally in 1694 the Bank of England was set up to provide sorely needed credit expansion. Early credit expansion was in the form of paper currency. Such currency made more economical use of the gold supply, but the fractional reserve ratio was fairly high, so that the monetary system was still largely inflexible. The extended use of checks made possible an even lower fractional reserve ratio, and later the phenomenal expansion of credit in the form of government bonds and Treasury loans so extended the elasticity of the monetary conveyance that it could easily be enlarged at will to accommodate any growth in production. The monetary conveyance of the modern era will again be discussed; consequently further consideration may be deferred until then. It is sufficient to note at this point that the English did evolve a satisfactory monetary conveyance.

The fifth conveyance, an adequate transportation and communication system, was eminently present in the English economy. Moreover, the middle class through its individualistic efforts soon improved it vastly. One of the important features of the English industrial revolution was the improvement in transportation and communication.

Yet, with all these favorable factors, there was a definite limit to which the English industrial revolution could proceed. The democracy which evolved in the earlier stages of the industrial revolution was restrictive in some measure. It permitted sufficient freedom to the industrial capitalists to break down the mercantilist tradition, but the caste system endured. Adam Smith provided the powerful intellectual argument which the industrial capitalists needed in their struggle with the merchant capitalists. An emotional wave of liberalism, influenced no doubt by the American tradition and the French Revolution, swept through all the English classes. Restrictive laws and regulations on trade and commerce were removed, and the enterprising industrial capitalists were allowed almost complete freedom in their efforts to evolve the factory system.

Limitations of the Industrial Revolution in England

Yet, because the caste system endured, the exploitive viewpoint of the upper classes was adopted readily by the industrial capitalists. The Malthusian theory of population rested upon a peculiar basic assumption which was a carry-over from the feudalistic era. It assumed that the human society was made up of two distinct classes, an upper class and a lower class. Moreover, the distinction between these two classes was assumed to be so great that the forces governing the reproduction rate were supposed to be entirely different for each. According to the theory in its most naïve form, the upper class exercised restraint upon its population increase without economic coercion, whereas the lower class exercised no cultural restraint and therefore could be contained only by economic scarcity. Thomas Malthus introduced a number of more sophisticated qualifications to the theory, but the basic assumption of class distinction was not altered. The Malthusian theory provided the intellectual argument for a subsistence theory of wages, by which industrial capitalists justified a low wage for factory workers. The wages fund theory and, later, the marginal productivity theory of wages were successive retirements from an intellectual position which proved untenable as the cultural level of the lower class was improved. The surplus value theory of Karl Marx represented a direct, frontal attack upon the entire basis for the classical and neoclassical wage theories. Marx recognized the class distinction and the exploitive viewpoint of the upper class. But he failed to recognize the potentialities of an individualistic middle class development. He classified all middle class individuals in the same category as the restrictive and monopolistic upper class, and thus missed the progressive spirit which individual initiative imparts to a society. In his mind there were only two groups, an upper class and a lower class—he paid little or no attention to the individualists in between who were in the process of moving from the lower to the upper category, and who in so doing were exerting a dynamic influence upon the civilization. He saw the societal friction only as a clash between two distinct groups, the exploiters and the exploited. The individual did not count. It is not surprising that he failed to understand the fundamental strength of the democratic spirit.

As a result of the partial continuation of class distinction, and the consequent partial adaptation of the exploitive technique, the system of privileges and monopolies was imperfectly broken down. Moreover, successful middle class individualists found it easy in such an atmosphere to build up new privileges and restrictions as soon as they had gained positions which were worth protecting. Thus, while conditions for an original upsurge of middle class activity were favorable enough to bring about an industrial revolution, the conditions necessary for a continuation of unrestricted middle class activity were less satisfactory, and as a consequence the era of rapid change and development soon gave way to an era of trusts and monopolies.

England pioneered in the initial phases of economic expansion and change through industrial capitalism. She also planted the seeds for a continuation of middle class growth in the colonial areas. But the restrictive elements introduced by an incomplete destruction of the caste system limited the extent to which the newborn industrialization process could proceed. In a period of rapid change capital equipment ordinarily becomes obsolescent long before it is actually worn out. But when industrial capitalists combine to fix prices and to share the market, the competitive forces are so weakened that capital equipment may be kept in use long after equipment of similar design has become obsolescent in more progressive economies. England suffered from this experience. As a result her cost structure was kept rather high and she had increasing difficulty in meeting competitive forces in the world market. To help control the cost structure labor costs were held down, but this restriction on labor costs was insufficient to make up for the partial failure to keep productive techniques progressive. Also the lower wage structure meant that the internal market could not be cultivated as intensively as in societies where the middle class made up a large proportion of the total population. England evolved a system of standardization of machines, parts, and products. But she did not successfully attain the stage of mass production for the total market. She turned, rather, to quality production for a somewhat restricted market, although not in the extreme form in which France developed a highly restrictive system for a luxury market.

Because of the partial retention of the caste system and the consequent incomplete development of her middle class in the eighteenth and nineteenth centuries, England has moved on to the resolution of the conflict between the upper and lower classes without reaching the stage of complete mechanization. Less emphasis has come to be placed upon an expansion of total production than upon a more equitable distribution of the existing flow of production. Meanwhile, however, the rate of increase in the production itself has begun to shrink. The external markets have begun to fail as middle class activity in the overseas markets has brought about a more advanced system of industrialization in those areas. For a time England was able to maintain her imports from the overseas markets by living on the interest and dividends resulting from former investments abroad. But the heavy costs of warfare in the first half of the twentieth century have forced her to cash in many of these investments in return for immediate large-scale supplies of armaments.

Insofar as England has used her accumulation of wealth and privilege in overseas areas for immediate defense her position is analogous to that of the medieval nobles who sold their rights to the middle class townsmen or, at a later date, to that of the Spaniards who spent their accumulations of gold for consumption goods.

If that were the total picture, or if that were all that England had accomplished, her significance in the future world society would be small. But her individualistic middle class is by no means extinct, even though it is suffering serious losses at present from migration. This middle class continues to be sufficiently active to ensure the intellectual and cultural leadership of that country for some time to come. She is still engaged, as it were, in casting the seeds of her culture broadside throughout the world, and they are taking root not only in Anglo-Saxon countries but in many other areas as well. It may also be that the middle class individualists will again be able to push aside for a time many of the restrictive and institutionalized barriers which have been thrust up, and for a period we may see a revitalized and progressive English spirit at work. Whether such a revitalization process does occur or not, the English conveyances continue to be strong enough to ensure a continuation of active and powerful English leadership in all phases of human society.

CHAPTER SEVEN

The Second Industrial Revolution: II

Economic Forces in Early America

In the early colonial days a certain measure of class distinction was evident. Something resembling the caste system of England was transplanted to the American colonies. But the opportunities for middle class individualism were too great for caste monopoly and restriction to endure long. The revolt of the American colonies against England was distinctly a middle class revolt against such upper class privilege. Because the freedom was obtained by open conflict rather than by compromise, many restrictions which might otherwise have continued in vestigial form were swept away. The forces of democracy and individualism were given a free rein. As a result the techniques evolved by the English middle class in the first phase of the industrial revolution formed the basis for a second and more advanced development in the New World.

The most striking feature in the second or American phase of the industrial revolution was the emphasis upon production for the total market. Standardized and interchangeable parts made possible a highly diverse and complex system of specialization and division of labor. As the individual operations of production were simplified, mechanization of the processes was made possible. The amount of capital equipment used by each individual increased rapidly. The physical strength of the worker became less and less important, while the mental ability and training of the individual producer became more important. Enlightened self-interest led the industrial capitalists to encourage cultural and vocational training. (Each worker in the system was too important to ignore. One inadequately trained, disgruntled, or overtired man in a factory could do enormous damage in a brief period of time. It did not pay to hold down wages or to insist upon many hours of work each week.)

(The worker, therefore, obtained three important advantages which the English laborer had not had in similar proportions. These advantages were higher wages, more leisure, and broader opportunities for cultural and vocational training.) The society was now reaching down deeply into the lower class in order to bring up new additions to the middle class. Moreover, the investment in human material was paying high dividends in the form of inventions and innovations of every sort. The society was becoming increasingly eclectic, and was rapidly advancing to a higher, although temporarily materialistic, level of culture. The cultural advance was on two fronts: first, the boundaries of human knowledge were broadened by the intellectual leaders; and, second, the culture was rapidly being disseminated in more or less vulgarized form through all levels of the population.

The mass production technique led, however, to a centralization of business organization which operated to restrain individual initiative in some measure. Successful middle class individualists through corporate control sought to erect a new system of monopoly and privilege. Antitrust legislation has helped to contain this tendency in the American society, but the free play of competitive forces and that of individual initiative are definitely being restrained to a certain degree by the gradual growth of oligopoly and monopoly. Laboring groups also are seeking by collective action to counteract the growing power of the new capitalists. As in England the middle class individualist is suffering from increasing restrictions and narrowing opportunities brought about by the monopoly-minded upper and lower classes. The crystallization process is certainly less advanced in America than it is in England, but the trend is, nevertheless, clearly evident. It is interesting to note that both the upper classes, including the mercantilists, and the lower classes seek wherever possible to gain an advantage through legal sanction, while the middle class seeks always to keep government control out of the picture as much as possible.

Actually there are so many forces at work in the modern American society that a comprehensive interpretation would necessitate consideration of all the major fields of human activity. Since that cannot be attempted in this study, the assessment which is presented here and continued in the final chapter is necessarily inconclusive. Meanwhile, on the basis of the unitary causal theory which has been developed, it should be possible to examine some of the underlying factors which have brought about the modern business cycle. This phenomenon definitely falls within the purview of the present study.

What causes these economic pulsations? They are certainly man-made, since they originate in prosperous communities only, and operate separately from natural causes. In the nineteenth century economists paid little attention to them. At that time the emphasis was on intensive and extensive economic development and expansion. To enlarge and to diversify production, the total stock of capital had to be built up, and increased specialization of both labor and capital had to be encouraged. As much as possible had to be saved for reinvestment in industry if the highly efficient and roundabout system of capitalistic production was to be evolved. Movements within the labor force, accompanied by temporary disruptions for workers, were considered inevitable during such a period of change. The economists of that time considered that full employment was a natural state of affairs, and that any temporary slackening of output which resulted in unemployment would soon right itself as the existing industries adjusted, or as new industries developed and expanded. They assumed, of course, that the economy was competitive, and that wages and prices were flexible. They also assumed a high degree of mobility of capital and labor.

Actually the economists of that time were not unrealistic. The institutional conditions of the period were considerably different from those of the present. During the past hundred and fifty years a number of fundamental institutional changes have taken place which have an important bearing on modern business fluctuations. These changes were incipient in the nineteenth century, and therefore they attracted little notice by the economists of that period. Today they have assumed significant proportions, and should be examined carefully before proceeding to a consideration of the economic theory involved in the problem.

In 1800 approximately 85 per cent of the workers in the American economy were engaged in agriculture. Today the situation is almost exactly reversed. About 14 per cent are engaged in agriculture and 86 per cent in industrial production and various services. Perhaps in the not too distant future as few as 8 to 10 per cent of the workers will be able to provide the necessary agricultural output. It is true that in 1800 export surpluses were practically all in the form of agricultural and other extractive products. But even today there is normally a substantial agricultural surplus of certain products available for export.

The second fundamental change in the economy has been the growth of corporations. As long as most of the production was agricultural, and as long as the industrial production which did occur was on a fairly small scale for local markets, most business enterprises were operated by individuals on their own account. There was no need for large-scale concentration of capital in order to undertake industrial production. Even production of iron and steel items was carried out largely in small foundries and blacksmith shops. But, with the technological innovations arising from the industrial revolution, and with the expansion of markets to nation-wide and even international proportions, large amounts of capital had to be gathered in order to undertake industrial enterprise on the required scale. Some of this capital was obtained by plowing back profits from earlier production. A large amount of the initial capital was obtained, however, through incorporation and widespread sale of shares.

As a result of these two basic changes in the economy, namely, the trend toward industrialization and the growth of corporations, a third fundamental alteration has occurred. This is the phenomenal increase in the proportion of highly specialized wage and salary earners in the industrial and service areas. Most of these workers are only semiskilled, it is true; but they are highly specialized and to that extent immobilized.

In a given period agricultural output is determined for the most part by the forces of nature. Business fluctuations will affect agricultural prices, but employment in this area is ordinarily sustained. Even in the industrial and service areas continuity of employment and production is fairly well maintained as long as these business enterprises are operated by individuals on their own account. The money incomes of the proprietors rise or fall with business fluctuations and general economic conditions, while variations in the level of employment are not large, since individuals operating on their own account will continue to produce for a low money income rather than remain idle. Under these conditions fluctuations in prices and money incomes will be emphasized, whereas employment, real production, and real incomes will hold at a somewhat steadier level.

When a very large proportion of the workers are employed by corporations, the situation is quite different. The corporations, in their efforts to maximize money profits or to minimize money losses, are more disposed to raise or lower the level of output according to the demand for their products. Consequently fluctuations in real output and in employment are emphasized, while prices and wages of those who hold their jobs are somewhat inflexible downward.

An additional factor is that, where nearly all producers work for a wage or salary, there is a distinct loss of individualism. Instead of relying on his own powers and initiative to solve his economic problems, the worker learns to lean on the corporation by which he is employed. When economic conditions are adverse he may be spurred to extra effort by a desire to hold his job, but as long as he retains his position his personal economic problem is solved. If, however, he is one of the many who loses his job during a depression, he is usually quite helpless—and looks to the government to help him solve his economic problem. There are always some enterprising individuals, it is true, who may undertake to solve their own problems through personal effort and initiative. But such enterprising individuals are uncommon. They represent the exception rather than the rule. Indeed, the institutional conditions in the modern economy militate against personal enterprise, since the worker must be highly specialized and therefore dependent upon some institution in the society to provide him with employment. If he can find a corporation which will use his services, that solves his economic problem. He is fitted into the complex economy. Otherwise he looks to the government to provide employment or, as a last resort, purchasing power in the form of relief.

Because of these institutional changes the basic assumptions of the classical economists are no longer valid. Price competition in the sale of products and in the sale of labor is fading out. In its place we have a huge array of oligopolistic and monopolistic firms on the one hand, and of equally oligopolistic and monopolistic labor unions on the other. Even professional societies operate as monopolies wherever possible, and through restrictions on membership seek to maintain the level of professional fees. Prices and wages are no longer flexible downward. Also, because of the high degree of specialization in capital and labor, the mobility of these factors has been adversely affected.

When we examine the leading business cycle theories with these institutional factors in mind, we find that the theories form a unified and coherent pattern. The monetary theory is fundamental, and is interwoven in all the others. We may therefore consider certain aspects of the monetary theory first, and return to further consideration of it as necessary.

As far as the whole economy is concerned, money is a valuable conveyance. In money the concept of personal ownership is engendered and the spirit of individualism is fostered. Local loyalties in the form of prejudices, intolerances, and other irrational ways of thinking, are discouraged and partially broken down through the impersonal relationships of the market. Because money as real wealth or as a property right is compact and generally acceptable, holders of this asset enjoy certain individual and unique prerogatives arising from the wide range of choice and freedom of action. Moreover, a nonemotional rationale is provided whereby all goods and services are brought to a common denominator and equated on the basis of reason through the price system. Finally, money operates as a catalyst in the economy, facilitating an impersonal exchange of goods and services in the market.

From the viewpoint of the individual, money is the purpose of economic endeavor. Each worker performs some highly specialized task, and is rewarded in the form of money. He then uses his money income in three ways. He saves some, he pays taxes, and he buys goods and services for consumption.

But this technique of production for sale introduces a new complication with respect to investment. When production is for use the producer automatically invests his own savings. The farmer repairs his fences or builds new ones. The fisherman fashions items of tackle to further his own production. In doing so these workers replace and increase their personal stock of capital. But when a producer works for a money income he does not automatically or even necessarily invest his own savings. The money he saves is loan capital.[1] If he loans it out, from his viewpoint it is invested, but from the viewpoint of the economy as a whole the loaned money is still loan capital. Before it can become equity

[1] Norman J. Silberling, *Dynamics of Business* (New York: McGraw-Hill Book Company, 1939).

capital it must be invested by the borrower. The producer may invest it himself by buying capital items to further his own production, by buying shares in a corporation, or by otherwise helping to finance business enterprise. Or he may lend out his savings through the purchase of mortgages, life insurance, bonds, and the like. In the latter event the savings are invested by the borrowers.

But suppose the borrowers do not readily take up the available loan capital. Or suppose they want more than is being saved. Classical economists believed that the rate of savings and the rate of investment were equated through the interest rate. When the interest rate declined, the rate of savings decreased and the rate of investment increased. When the interest rate rose, the situation was reversed. It is possible that the interest rate may have had some such effect on savings in the nineteenth century, when savings habits were not yet institutionalized. But in the present economy, where corporations make it a practice to withhold a portion of profits to augment reserves, and where most savings of individuals are contractual, the rate of savings is more a function of the size and distribution of national income than of the interest rate. On the other hand, investment decisions are clearly affected by the interest rate, although the degree to which investment decisions are affected will vary inversely with necessary allowances for risk and uncertainty.

It would appear, therefore, that interest rates are an inadequate means for equating savings and investment. In fact, the experience of the 1930's would certainly confirm this conclusion. If the rate of voluntary investment exceeds the rate of savings, there is a shortage of loan capital, and the creation of purchasing power in excess of the real rate of savings causes an involuntary reduction of inventories. This is the inflationary gap.[2] An expansion of the circular flow in real or in money terms, or in both, then results. But, if the rate of savings exceeds the rate of voluntary investment, some of the loan capital becomes surplus. Lags begin to occur in the circular flow, causing an involuntary rise in

[2] These terms were developed by J. M. Keynes.

inventories and a slowing down of the circular flow. This is the deflationary gap.

Inflationary and deflationary gaps occur in a money economy only. They cannot occur in an economy where production is for use rather than for sale, and where savings therefore directly assume the form of equity capital.

If the economy fluctuates between inflation and deflation alternately, without undue emphasis upon either, we may conclude that the volume of savings over the business cycle is neither too large nor too small for the investment needs of the economy. If, on the other hand, the inflationary gap predominates, the rate of savings is insufficient for the rate of economic progress being attempted (government consumption expenditures may also create inflation); while if the deflationary gap predominates, the rate of savings is too high or the economy is not progressive enough.

When fluctuations in the level of voluntary investment are merely temporary phenomena, and do not indicate a chronic shortage of savings on the one hand, or a chronic shortage of investment opportunities on the other, the problem becomes one of adjustment only. When there is an inflationary gap, government capital expenditures may be held down; and when there is a deflationary gap, they may be increased substantially. The government capital budget is thus balanced over the period of the business cycle, instead of annually. The Swedish double budget system exemplifies this technique. The Keynesian solution is similar in some respects. But deliberate alternation of government capital expenditures is not a cure for persistent inflationary or deflationary tendencies in the economy. The cyclical budget is merely a counterbalancing technique.

As the principle of acceleration indicates, economic fluctuations in a growing economy are to be expected. Producers, particularly producers of capital goods, must build up their productive facilities to supply the net investment needs of the economy. Therefore, once economic growth is underway and the producers of capital goods become geared to the growth, a mere slowing down in the rate of the growth is sufficient to start a business cycle. True, there may have been some ignorance and shortsightedness on the part of the producers of capital goods. Perhaps they should have been more cautious in gearing up their productive facilities. But if they had failed to do so they might easily have lost their markets to more aggressive competitors. Also, in an economic system where production decisions are discrete and where the productive processes are highly complex and lengthy, future demand is very difficult to estimate.

In this connection it is interesting to note that supply in an industrial economy can easily be more elastic than demand. As the Cobweb Theorem indicates, this condition causes unstable equilibrium, and theoretically could lead to an explosive economy if other restraints were not present.[3] In practice the result is a chronic tendency to overproduce fixed capital, and, to a lesser degree, circulating capital. The flow of capital goods is then cut back until there is another upsurge in the demand for capital goods, as growth is resumed. The waves of overproduction and underproduction may be moderated through an improved knowledge of the total market, but in a growing economy the process of negative and positive acceleration is likely to operate under the best of circumstances.

Secular Stagnation

Thus far we have concentrated on the purely cyclical aspects of business fluctuations. The next step is to consider certain of the trend aspects. Of course, the problem of secular stagnation ranks first in this field.[4]

[3] Sellers are encouraged to push the demand curve to the right by searching out new markets, and by extensive advertising. See Appendix.

[4] Alvin H. Hansen, *Readings in Business Cycle Theory* (Philadelphia: Blakiston Company, 1944), Art. 18. J. M. Keynes also considers the problem briefly in his book, *The General Theory of Employment, Interest and Money* (London: Macmillan & Co., Ltd., 1936), pp. 324-326.

According to the secular stagnation thesis, opportunities for profitable investment are not keeping pace with the rate of savings. Savings in excess of depreciation needs go to increase the size of the capital stock. But the increase in capital stock results, after a gestation period, in an enlarged flow of production.

It is this extra production which creates the problem. Unless we begin to consume more at once, or unless the extra production which is not consumed goes into investments to build up the stock of capital even further, some of this production becomes surplus. As we build up total production we increase our expenditure on consumption goods and services. But the increase in consumption often lags behind the increase in the flow of production. This means a rising rate of savings, and an enlarged volume of loan capital available for investment.

But, according to the stagnation thesis, opportunities for profitable investment are dwindling, even while the amount of loan capital is increasing. The threat of depression becomes greater, and the pressure on the government to spend the excess savings through deficit financing becomes chronically more persistent.

Secular stagnationists point out that, from the discovery of the New World until early in the twentieth century, new opportunities for profitable investment were constantly opening up. While temporary crises and sharp depressions did occur, they automatically cured themselves. Unemployed workers, particularly the younger ones, drifted toward the geographic frontier where economic opportunities were more attractive. This solved the problem of employment. Also, in the building up of frontier areas large volumes of fixed capital were needed. Surplus savings in the older communities therefore flowed into frontier investments or into new plant and equipment to supply frontier needs. To provide for geographic expansion there had to be savings in excess of depreciation allowances.

But, with the disappearance of the frontier, opportunities

for further economic growth are more limited. Therefore, a smaller proportion is needed for net investment. In simple terms, the secular stagnationists argue that, as our economy matures, we should save less and consume more.

If the rate of growth in the economy is indeed slowing down, the secular stagnation thesis and its implications are of prime importance. Yet, some economists are of the opinion that there is still a limitless economic frontier to be explored—the intensive or innovation frontier.[5]

According to this argument, innovations can create limitless opportunities for further economic growth and profitable net investment. The use of steam power gave rise to the innovations of railroads and steamships, thereby creating an enormous need for net investment. The creation of power through internal combustion made possible the innovation of automobiles. Today, the discovery of atomic energy through nuclear fission opens up new vistas of economic expansion. (As long as we can continue to progress through our creative powers, there seems to be little question about the possibilities of economic growth, and the need for continued net investment.)

The really serious economic problem arises from the fact that innovations do not proceed at a regular pace. They occur, rather, in fits and starts. Moreover, the incentive to work out and to use innovations for profit is greater during prosperous periods than during depression. Consequently, periods of prosperity are strengthened, whereas during depression we hesitate to try what might appear to be a worth-while undertaking when economic conditions are favorable.

There have to be some apparent need for innovations and a good possibility of profit in order to bring them forth. But with the disappearance of the geographic frontier, the opportunities for economic growth in expansive terms have become more

---

[5] Joseph Schumpeter, *Business Cycles* (New York: McGraw-Hill Book Company, 1939); and Knut Wicksell, *Interest and Prices* (London: Macmillan & Co., Ltd., 1936), Chap. XI.

limited. The geographic frontier encouraged transportation and communications innovations. Warfare stimulates innovations in techniques of offense and defense. With the passing of the geographic frontier, our problem is how to stimulate a flow of further innovations without constantly having to revert to warfare. The prosperity of the 1940's and early 1950's was definitely war-made. Can we create similar conditions in peacetime? We have not yet solved this problem. Meanwhile, the secular stagnation thesis continues to haunt us.

The Middle Class Ethic

We are so accustomed to living in an economy where a substantial amount of income is saved that we find it hard to think of a different kind of economy. Yet, in a historical sense, our economy is unusual. During most periods of history there was very little net investment. In fact, periods of negative net investment or economic degeneration have not been uncommon. Until quite recently we have been most sporadic in building up our economic strength.[6]

When we examine the general attitude of the upper classes in the medieval period, we get some idea of the significant change which has taken place. In the Middle Ages a gentleman did not engage in economic production. To do so would have been degrading. Although he did not cultivate long fingernails in the manner of the Chinese upper classes, he was required by custom and tradition to engage in "honorable" activities only—such activities as fighting, dueling, sports, gambling, religious exercises, and government. He might pursue intellectual activities if he wished; but ordinarily he was a dilettante, interested in fine figures of speech, poetry, and perhaps scholastic forms of logic. He

[6] The leading works in this field are Max Weber, *The Protestant Ethic and the Spirit of Capitalism* (New York: Oxford University Press, 1948); Werner Sombart, *The Quintessence of Capitalism* (London: Macmillan & Co., Ltd., 1915); and Thorstein Veblen, *The Theory of the Leisure Class* (New York: Modern Library, n.d.).

was so completely divorced from the mundane activities of economic life that his occasional intellectual excursions were rarely of pragmatic significance.

It is true that there were middle class individualists who were busy building up their personal fortunes in trade, commerce, and industry. But they were yet too few in numbers to have more than a minor influence on the economy of that time. They were in the process of building themselves up in preparation for the commercial and industrial revolutions they were to bring about later. Meanwhile the upper classes were still in control. And tradition discouraged capable members of the upper classes from saving, from producing, and from engaging in intellectual pursuits which might have improved the economy. They spent the proceeds of their estates with a lavish hand, regarded productive activity as a slavish undertaking, and looked upon serious study as a fit occupation for the junior cleric only.

Slowly and insidiously at first, and then more swiftly as they gained in numbers and economic strength, the middle class individualists became predominant in the society. As this occurred, the old ruling classes were pushed aside, and the middle class ethic became the ethical standard for the whole society. In America today we are a middle class people—even more so than in European countries where vestiges of the old upper classes still remain.

Since we are a middle class people, it is important that we understand the nature and implications of our own ethics. In the first place, we believe it is virtuous to save part of our income. In our society the individual who spends all of his income is regarded somewhat as a waster, a ne'er-do-well. Moreover, heads of corporations adopt the same attitude with respect to corporate profits. While we have greatly expanded our consumption expenditures as we have improved our productive efficiency, there is a tendency for the increase in consumption to lag behind the growth in production.

We also believe it is virtuous to be industrious. Idleness is frowned upon in our society. A wealthy individual who does not work is usually labeled as a playboy or "gentleman of leisure." His activities make good material for the newspapers, but underlying such popular interest there is definite social disapproval. Because we are middle class-minded, America is a society where millionaires go to work, as well as everyone else.

The habit of saving and the habit of industriousness go hand in hand. By saving we build our stock of capital; through industry we use the capital to increase the flow of production. As a result of the two actions our economic position is improved. But in the process we are sometimes disposed to forget that the primary purpose of the thrift and industry is to improve our level of consumption. The thrift and the industry are means to an end, not ends in themselves. We are so bound by the customs and traditions of our middle class ethic that we may be in danger of forgetting this simple truth. The individual who has saved and striven in the economic sphere for many years finds it very hard to turn from economic pursuits and to enjoy the fruits of his labor. He hardly knows how to increase his rate of consumption, or how to direct his newfound leisure into noneconomic activities.

As long as the habit of industriousness keeps pace with thrift, the savings in the form of loan capital flow readily into investment in the form of equity capital. Middle class intellectual pursuits make an important contribution in this respect. Because many of the intellectual activities are directed into pragmatic channels, innovations which will absorb the savings are promoted and developed. But no amount of pragmatic research can keep pace with savings which mount at an accelerating pace.

An economy which has too small a volume of savings in proportion to population can experience unemployment and economic hardship because of a shortage of fixed and circulating capital with which to work. Italy and perhaps Japan seem to be plagued by this problem. An economy which has too large a volume of savings can have unemployment and depression because of a surplus of loan capital. In the first case there is a lack of

physical means of production; in the second case there are adequate means of production and an ample number of workers, but
there is a lack of effective demand. The rate of savings has out-
stripped profitable investment opportunities.

Many of the Western democracies, and America in particular,
are chronically faced with the second problem. Quite evidently
we have allowed the middle class ethic to get out of hand. Like
the individual who has saved and striven for many years, we, as a
society, find it hard to increase our rate of consumption com-
mensurately with the growth in our production.

The classical economists of the nineteenth century concentrated on the economics of production. Perhaps twentieth century economists should place greater emphasis on the economics
of demand.

Monetary Theory

At this point we may return to further consideration of the
monetary theory. In this connection there are two problems
which should be noted. The first is the maintenance of a monetary
flow which will match the growth in the flow of production. The
second is the problem arising from the liquidity preference. Finally, this problem will serve as an introduction to the role of
privilege and restriction in our society.

If the flow of money expands more slowly than the flow of
goods and services, the money becomes relatively scarce and the
general price level is depressed. Producers are discouraged from
further productive effort, since their profits are constantly being
squeezed. The money they get for their production is more valuable, it is true; but contractual obligations involved in the productive process and increased difficulties encountered in getting
back to a liquid position each time production is attempted may
mean that they get back from the sale of their products little
more than they put in as costs. Quite evidently an adequate

monetary system is essential for sustained middle class activity. Where the growth in the monetary flow proceeds at a slightly faster rate than the growth in the flow of production, prices are buoyant and middle class activity is sustained or even intensified. But the excess growth in the flow of money must not proceed too fast; otherwise, confidence in the money conveyance may be adversely affected.

There are three ways in which the money supply can grow. First, new gold and silver may be mined. Second, the credit structure may be expanded. Third, gold may be periodically revalued at a higher rate in monetary terms. Historically, all three methods have been used. Actually, the third method is the most clearcut and easy to control, since the money supply is thereby made sufficiently flexible without rendering it unstable. An added advantage is that it stimulates production of new gold and silver to meet the needs for an enlarged monetary supply. But this solution assumes adherence to the gold standard and brings to the fore many complications in connection with international trade.

When trading nations are on the gold standard three basic conditions must be met if chronic disequilibrium is to be avoided. First, competitive forces in international trade must be reasonably active. Second, tariffs, exchange controls, and other barriers must not interfere unduly with the flow of goods and services. Third, countries which have a sufficient superiority in productive efficiency must be prepared to invest net export balances abroad. During the latter half of the nineteenth century, even though she had free trade, England had an export surplus. Yet, there was no serious shortage of sterling currency in the world market because these net exports were invested abroad. But in the twentieth century the United States, through a combination of productive superiority and trade barriers, has had a persistent net export surplus which she has not invested abroad. As a result, the gold flow to the United States reached such proportions in the first half of the century that the international gold standard had to be abandoned. In more recent years our net export surplus has been maintained through loans and gifts abroad. This technique is purely a palliative and does not solve the problem.

There are some trends which may bring about a basic change. First, we are beginning to run short of certain materials, and must look abroad for supplies. In order to build up and to maintain the necessary flow of these materials from foreign sources, investment abroad must be undertaken. Second, many of the expanding oligopolies and monopolies are reaching the end of the national market and must look abroad for further expansion of sales. A struggle between expansive oligopolies and monopolies who are becoming internationally minded and restrictive oligopolists and monopolists who favor restriction and exploitation within the national market is already becoming evident. Also, the population is still growing rapidly, and while agrarian advances have thus far kept pace, the population growth may reach the point where certain basic foodstuffs have to be imported.

Meanwhile the expansion of the credit structure to meet the need for a larger money supply has created the serious problem of monetary instability, which central banking activities have not been able to overcome. Also, since there is no true basis for a limitation on the expansion of credit money, confidence in such money is not assured.

There is, of course, nothing sacred about gold or silver as money standards. An adequate but stable money system based on a managed paper currency is theoretically quite feasible. But the proper management of such a currency and such a credit structure presumes a clear understanding of the abstractions involved. The orthodox interpretation is to think of credit expansion and contraction in terms of commercial bank loans and central banking activities. But the volume and nature of government credit are also fundamental.

If excess government expenditures arising from deficit financing enlarge the volume of government credit so that the flow of money in the economy increases at about the same rate that the flow of production increases, the extra money supply is justified and necessary. But when excess government expenditures enlarge the flow of money at a much faster pace than the growth in the flow of production, the result is purely inflationary.

Unfortunately, many monetary theorists are disposed to overlook this fundamental danger because the disastrous effects are not always immediately evident. The creation of vast new quantities of government credit may proceed long past the safety mark before the gross overexpansion of the monetary structure becomes noticeable. When the new government credit is held by individuals and firms in the form of bonds or short-term securities, the potential expansion in the money flow is latent. The government has merely put back into circulation purchasing power in the form of loan capital which these individuals and firms did not elect to use.

But the very existence of this new government credit constitutes a threat to the monetary system. If the government credit in the form of bonds or securities gets into the hands of the commercial banks, it is immediately monetized. The volume of bank credit rises just as if commercial loans had been expanded. If the government credit passes into the hands of the central bank, the inflationary effects are multiplied. Commercial bank reserves increase by the same amount, and therefore an expansion of bank credit through the fractional reserve system is made possible.

To maintain confidence in the public debt the government must be prepared at all times to liquefy individual holdings through an extension of bank credit, or as a last resort, through purchase by the central bank. The government can, of course, permit its bonds to go to some discount in the open market; but, insofar as it does so, bond conversions must be made at higher rates of interest. On a sophisticated level, the persistent issue of new government credit at a rate faster than the growth in the flow of production constitutes a debasement of the monetary system in the same way that debasement of actual coins in Rome or printing of new paper money constituted a debasement in Germany and more recently in China.

The other facet to the monetary interpretation is the liquidity preference. As we noted earlier, from the viewpoint of the society as a whole, money is merely a conveyance whereby the flow of production is facilitated and enlarged through specialization and division of labor. As far as the society is concerned, goods and services are invested and exchanged as factors of production, and as a consequence there is an enlarged flow of finished goods and services. But from the viewpoint of the individual or business firm the situation is quite the reverse. For the individual the starting point is money, and liquidity is given up through investment in goods and services so that the ultimate stock of money held by the individual may be enlarged. For the individual the final sale of the product is the objective. He proceeds from a given stock of money through investment to an enlarged stock of money. Production on his part is only a means to that end. Consequently, if he can enlarge his liquid assets without producing, that is, by lending or by pirating, or if he can sell poor quality production at a profit, or if he can create an artificial scarcity of his product and thereby get high prices for it, he is encouraged to do so. Financial success, not quality and quantity of production, is the criterion by which the individual is judged, and he learns to respond accordingly. Materialism and unscrupulous tactics become the mode.

Decline of Middle Class Activity

As long as it is to the advantage of the middle class individualists to thrust aside privileges and restrictions so that they may gain their ends, they will favor the free play of competitive forces. But when a sufficient number of them attain a measure of success so that they have a preferred position to defend, they will favor collective action to maintain privileged positions. In other words, when the groups which favor privilege get enough reinforcements from the ranks of successful middle class individualists, and become strong enough to restrain the new individualistic rule breakers, economic progress slows down.

At the present time, management and labor are both moving toward collectivism. Both favor governmental restrictions which will aid their special interests, and both oppose governmental restrictions which might restrain their privileges. Meanwhile the true middle class individualist, who favors as little governmental intervention as possible, is slowly being squeezed between the collectivists.

According to this interpretation of the role of privilege, business fluctuations are more than a series of ups and downs, more than cyclical manifestations; they indicate a trend. Apart from the influence on innovations and the influence on credit expansion imparted by warfare, if the interpretation is valid we may expect to see a chronic tendency toward ever greater depressions. To keep the system operating, government intervention then becomes inevitable. During prosperous periods or during war, or both, prices are pushed up. When depression threatens, a return to the old price level would cause serious trade dislocations, battles with labor groups, and wholesale unemployment. The government is under enormous public pressure to prevent this. New government credit is issued through deficit financing to replenish the effective demand. As a consequence, there is an intermittent debasement of the monetary system, a squeezing out of competitive forces, and a gradual slowing down of economic growth and expansion.

CHAPTER EIGHT

Penultimate Generalizations

Recapitulation

The factors which must be favorable for the development of a vigorous middle class are (1) a sufficiently strong central government to assure the maintenance of law and order in the trading area, (2) a reasonable measure of religious and political toleration (too much latitude here endangers the cohesion of the society and brings about a lack of balance in the culture), (3) limitation of warfare to areas outside the home territory, (4) an adequate but stable form of money, (5) adequate transportation and communication facilities, and (6) the development of a democratic tradition wherein individualism may flourish.

The outstanding phases in the development and decline of a society are (1) a primitive, communal mode of life, (2) the emergence of a barbaric ruler-slave state, (3) the growth of feudalism, (4) an age of tyrants, (5) emergence of a full-fledged middle class under democracy, (6) an expansion of the middle class to include some of the proletariat. At any time after the fourth phase a society may revert to an authoritarian form. When this occurs the society moves on toward its more or less lengthy period of universality, staticism, and eventual breakdown. The growth of authoritarianism occurs when privilege and restriction have so expanded that further middle class activity is stifled. The yeast in the society ceases to act, and the society ceases to develop to a higher level of culture, although the culture may for a time be enriched through refinements. Eventual decay and collapse then become merely a question of time, for no society can remain static in perpetuity.

Uses of Wealth and Levels of Culture

With respect to the various uses to which production can be put, the ultimate stage has not yet been reached in full measure. Suppose we review these uses. Production may be used for immediate consumption. The bulk of all production must, of course, be used for this purpose, since this is the ultimate purpose for which wealth is created. Yet, an examination into the forms which immediate consumption takes can provide insight into the level of the culture. Basic consumption might be termed instinctive; but even among primitive peoples many forms of consumption are sufficiently refined and sophisticated to require an acculturalization process for their development. The use of ornaments, for example, presupposes a certain social way of thinking. Often the ornaments denote social rank or have religious significance, or both. In other words, they have cultural meaning and their very existence provides a valuable clue to the form of the culture.

But, quite apart from the forms which immediate consumption may take, the fundamental economic difference between primitive peoples and civilized peoples is that civilized peoples have developed uses for wealth beyond those related to immediate consumption. It is true that primitive peoples will learn how to fashion simple items for production purposes, but for the most part such activities are undertaken to meet the exigencies of the moment only. Primitive peoples are sporadic in their productive activities, are almost childishly pragmatic, and do not look far ahead. If their supply of food or other necessaries fails for even a short period of time, a crisis develops. Frequently the rotation of the seasons is sufficient to force them to move about in search of food. Under such circumstances an abnormal season can be catastrophic for them, and can easily result in a complete change in the geographic location of the society, in the form of the culture, or in both.

The second use of wealth is storage for later disposition. The deliberate use of wealth for this purpose requires definite foresight. It is a form of provision for the future which primitive peoples cannot seem to appreciate fully. In deliberating the storing of wealth the producer is disciplining himself in three ways. He must produce consistently even though he has no immediate need for such production; he must overcome a natural inclination to use in a wasteful manner those forms of wealth which happen to be present in abundance at that point of time; and, third, he must plan and prepare the means for storage of wealth which is currently in excess of his needs. In other words, he has to visualize clearly what his needs are going to be over a period of time; he no longer lives like a child in the present only.

Some animals instinctively prepare for the future. Bees gather honey, squirrels store nuts, but man does none of these things through instinct. He does them deliberately and rationally. Through actual or vicarious experience he learns the necessity of preparing for the future, and forms a pattern of behavior for continued existence over a period of time.

Suppose we consider the three factors involved in the storage of wealth. Persistent production even when there is no present need for such production quite evidently increases the total amount produced over time. Instead of operating on the basis of mood, the members of the society discipline their activities and learn to coordinate their productive efforts. A definite pattern of production is worked out to allow for the seasonal changes and other geographical factors. By adhering to this customary pattern of behavior, even without much thought about it, the members of the society get into the habit of producing on a regular basis regardless of present need.

During harvest periods when particular types of foods are available in abundance, it is quite natural for the members of the society to consume the abundant forms freely. For the time being these items are somewhat in the nature of free economic goods. But the capacity of the human stomach is limited at any particular point of time, and for most items the festivity forms of consumption do not make serious inroads into the total supply. But the members of the society must discipline themselves against protracted orgies. Not only is the wastage which occurs during such orgies a serious loss; the time consumed in them is also very important. The whole of the harvest must be gathered while it is available; otherwise the greater part of it may be lost. Concentration upon complete exploitation of the harvest requires a form of discipline which primitive peoples find it hard to impose upon themselves. Again, the habit of productive effort when there is no present need for it must be fully developed. Civilized man must keep his eyes on the future at all times for his enlightened self-interest.

Storage of wealth for later use brings into being a need for an organized system of storage and a demand for the physical facilities for the storage, such as pits, bins, granaries. Derived demand for occupational forms of wealth expands and becomes an important part of the total demand in the economy.

Historically, the use of wealth for storage brought into existence many small communities along river valleys, such as the Nile, the Tigris and the Euphrates, and along lake shores. Here the soil was fertile and production easy, and here in their very early stages civilizations began to take form.

Systematic conquest and exploitation bring about the next stage in the development of civilization. The third use of wealth is the building up of arms for deliberate conquest. When wealth is stored it may later be used for consumption only, or it may simultaneously serve as a means for the production of new wealth. In the latter event the stored wealth is capital. But when arms are built up for the deliberate purpose of conquest, the arms represent a definite investment whereby the potential conquerors hope to gain new wealth through exploitation. They are not particularly interested in creating new wealth but rather in appropriating the wealth of the conquered peoples. Nevertheless, conquest of this type usually does bring about the creation of new wealth. It is therefore correct to say that arms for conquest are a form of capital.

The question arises as to how the new wealth is created. When the many small communities are integrated into one large kingdom, the law of comparative advantage can operate on a larger scale than before. Specialization and the division of labor become much more widespread and are intensified, and, as a result, the flow of production is increased. The state of technology has been improved by the superior form of productive organization. With the more complex structure of the productive system, the society has to look even farther ahead, and has to prepare itself accordingly. The economic organization becomes more capitalistic, more indirect, and more efficient.

But this does not mean that the social welfare is improved. Historical records would indicate that the situation has been quite the reverse. With the formation of the kingdom an entirely new type of society comes into existence. Control of the society and responsibility for its direction passes from the hands of the chieftains and elders and is placed in the hands of the king and his satellites, who lack personal ties with the people they rule. In fact, for the most part they are likely to regard such people as conquered slaves permitted to live on sufferance, provided they toil unceasingly in the interests of their masters. Under such circumstances the social welfare is, if anything, worse than when the people lived in small and autonomous communities.

Yet productivity is higher. There is now some surplus production above subsistence. Much of this surplus is appropriated by the ruling class and used for self-aggrandizement. But not all of it is squandered uselessly in such conspicuous consumption. Some goes into improvements in transportation and irrigation and into the application of such subjects as mathematics or astronomy. Even though the lot of the great majority is unhappy, the level of the culture continues to rise.

The fourth use of wealth comes into existence when capital is built up for trading purposes. Trading capital is often called merchant capital. Through trade the law of comparative advantage is permitted to operate over even greater geographic areas; also, within the given area, specialization and division of labor are further intensified. The use of wealth for trading purposes marks one of the great steps forward in man's economic mastery over his environment. As we have noted, this use of wealth is developed, not by the rulers and not by the slaves, but by an entirely new class of people—the middle class.

The fifth use of wealth is the unique contribution of the Western European culture. It is the use of wealth for industrial purposes. The use of industrial wealth promotes efficiency in production through increased specialization and division of labor. But this is only part of the story. Muscular strength and physical agility are required less and less. Machines now do this type of work on an ever-increasing scale. The worker comes to be valued more and more for what he knows and less and less for his physical capacities. Mechanical power, varied and highly complex materials, and machinery to perform the fabricating processes are the forms which industrial capital assumes. The mental skill of the worker in directing the new mechanical forces and processes is the important feature. The old hierarchy of highly skilled craftsmen and unskilled laborers fades out and is replaced by a new hierarchy of highly skilled technicians and semiskilled assembly-line workers. The ruler-slave concept recedes even further into the background, since there is now ample potential production for all. For a time the possibility of exploitation of natural forces replaces the emphasis upon exploitation of other human beings.

There is one more use of wealth—a use which we have not really mastered as yet. The intelligent use of wealth for social investment requires an exceedingly broad and clear comprehension of the abstractions involved. Long-range foresight is needed. When we use wealth to produce new wealth, we need to have some system of measurement to determine whether a particular investment is likely to be worth our while. The cost of arms for conquest can be measured against the booty which may be obtained. The trader can compare the cost of his merchandise and other expenses with the expected selling price. The industrial capitalist can divide the cost of the machine into the units of production which a machine may be expected to turn out during its period of usefulness, and thus obtain an estimation of unit costs for comparison with expected unit selling price. But the measurement of profit from social investment is not so easy to obtain.

There are a number of reasons why social investment defies ordinary means for measuring its efficiency. In the first place, the investment may take a long time to mature. Even though the eventual returns may be very large, private investors are not likely to be interested, partly because the human lifetime is limited and partly because, with the short business horizon, rapid discounting of future returns is encouraged so that such discounting may easily exceed the interest rate. Consequently, although large corporations may look far enough ahead to engage in some forms of social investment, much social investment has to be undertaken by governments. Soil conservation and reforestation are typical examples. The government is interested not only in the welfare of this generation, but also in the generations to follow. It can afford to wait for a return on its investment.

A second reason why social investment defies ordinary means for measuring its efficiency is that the returns often assume unpredictable forms. The investment may be made with one purpose in mind, whereas the results of the investment may accomplish quite a different purpose. As long as the purpose accomplished is sufficiently desirable the investment may be worth-while, but the unpredictable factor is disturbing. The society definitely benefits when a worth-while result is obtained; yet when an individual makes the social investment he is not always in a position to profit from an unpredictable result.

A third reason for the difficulty of measuring the returns from social investment is the fact that the market value tells only part of the story. We might say without hesitation that social investment in the scientific education of Louis Pasteur paid big dividends. But how much? To what extent in monetary terms has the society benefited from the discovery of preventive vaccination against rabies, vaccination of sheep against anthrax, and pasteurization of milk? The nonmarket values of these techniques are also of some importance.

Some aspects of social investment are more amenable to measurement than others. Accomplishments in the natural sciences in particular are manifested in rather tangible forms and the benefits are often immediately evident. Consequently investment in natural scientific research is made quite readily. Many large corporations maintain research laboratories because they have learned from experience that discoveries in the natural sciences obtained in this way are profitable. Many of the findings are the result of planned research. Occasionally, however, there may be unpredicted results. The corporations are large enough to accept this situation; they are ever ready to exploit results, planned or unplanned.

But social investment in the natural sciences is almost always pragmatic. Because basic research does not provide immediate and tangible results it is largely neglected. We have not learned to look that far ahead. In the social sciences the problem of social investment is even more acute. The results of social scientific research are rarely tangible and very seldom have immediate application. Where social research is attempted it is almost always for the purpose of solving some pressing social problem. Basic social research is practically virgin territory.

Social investment can be divided into a number of categories.

First, there is social overhead. In order to have an industrial society there must be investment in transportation, housing, schools, churches, hospitals, and other normal facilities for modern living. An industrial capitalist may make some of the investments in social overhead, but many of them are made by governments. Second, there is social investment in the intangibles—health, education. Third, there is social investment in the expansion of knowledge. This may be in the form of improved techniques, as noted above when we discussed pragmatic research, or it may take the form of basic research. It is evident that there is considerable overlapping between social overhead and the various forms of social investment in intangibles.

If we can attain sufficiently broad comprehension and foresight to develop the use of wealth for social investment on an extensive scale, the ultimate increase in the flow of production and the improvement of the social welfare of the total population may be substantial. It could easily overshadow all the previous economic developments and raise our culture to levels we can hardly conceive today.

Social investment is a two-edged tool. We need to analyze it thoroughly and to use it with great care if we are to derive the maximum benefit from it, and if we are to avoid damaging results which may accrue from its improper use. Both tangible and intangible forms of social investment are closely akin to the use of wealth for immediate consumption. Improved highways, housing, and various public works add to our immediate satisfactions. Improved health and understanding through education are also a source of satisfaction. These immediate satisfactions are desirable, for they improve our general standard of living. Yet, if they become the sole purpose of the social expenditures, the social investment program may easily degenerate into a giveaway program and thus become self-defeating.

Social investment is properly a form of capital investment. Unless it brings about the creation of new wealth it fails to fulfill this criterion, and is merely a form of immediate consumption.

Expenditures on tangible public projects and on improvement of the people are for the purpose of helping us to produce more efficiently. The fact that these public projects and improved human welfare add to our immediate satisfactions must not blind us to the additional fact that we are socially obligated to use our improved powers to produce to full advantage.

The Roman demagogues placated the Roman mob by providing free food and free entertainment, but such social expenditure did not result in an increase in total production. In fact, the members of the Roman mob were encouraged and abetted in their wasteful and idle habits. This type of social expenditure actually brings about a decrease in the flow of production, since it encourages idleness and waste. Social investment must be in such a form that we are encouraged to help ourselves. In other words, it must arouse latent creative urges.

In formulating programs of social investment there are a number of sound criteria by which to measure probable efficiency. First, social investment in potential producers is always worth-while, provided it improves abilities and stimulates creative activity. In practical terms, this means that large-scale investment in the health and education of children is socially desirable. Assistance to aged or incapacitated producers can also be justified both on humanitarian grounds, that is, to provide immediate satisfactions, and also as an investment. Many aged or incapacitated people have substantial contributions which they can and want to make if given the proper assistance and opportunity.

Social investment in actual producers is the real problem. Ill-calculated social expenditures for the benefit of actual producers can be very damaging to the morale of the individual and can operate to the disadvantage of the society. Yet, just because they are producers, human beings need not stop learning and improving themselves mentally and physically. There are always latent capacities to be developed and improvements to be made in physical welfare. How social expenditures for these purposes can be carried out so that creative activity is always stimulated requires careful examination and analysis.

In our society we have reached what might be termed a culminating and at the same time a turning point. By looking further and further ahead we have attained a high measure of efficiency in production. The greatly enlarged volume of production per capita enables us to have a high standard of living. If we now turn our attention to various forms of immediate consumption without regard to the future, we will be neglecting improvements in productive efficiency, and the productive system in operation now may well degenerate. But if we seek to look even further ahead and to prepare ourselves accordingly, we can move up to a yet higher level of efficiency, even while we are enjoying the fruits of past and present achievements. Immediate consumption provides satisfactions, but creative activity is also satisfying in itself, and there is no reason why we should deny ourselves this added form of satisfaction while we are enjoying various forms of immediate consumption.

In economics our concern is limited to problems relating to production for the market, since we take into account value in exchange only. Nevertheless, it should be noted that production which satisfies any of the six wants—basic needs, desires for variety in basic needs, conventional wants, occupational wants, aesthetic or spiritual wants, and egoistic wants—is creative. Some of these satisfactions, particularly those connected with aesthetic or spiritual desires, may not enter the market. Yet, in the broader social interpretation they may be considered equally important. To put it simply, not all production can be measured adequately in monetary terms.

Little Great-Man Thesis

Within recent years it has become fashionable among intellectuals to repudiate the great-man thesis of history. The repudiation of the thesis is in one sense very healthy. Emphasis has come to be placed upon the activities and contributions of less spectacular but nonetheless important elements within societies. Unfortunately, however, the fad appears to be going to the opposite extreme. If carried to the ultimate, a denial of the great-man thesis becomes a denial of self-determination. Human societies then become mere flotsam on the river of time to be carried helplessly along according to the currents and eddies which play upon them. Implicit in this study has been the thesis that individuals in a society are governed by the conveyances and loyalties which exist during their lifetime, but that individuals are by no means helpless on that account. Within the framework of the society the individual may not only seize opportunities; he may also make opportunities to alter and rearrange the society to match his desires. Societies pass through fairly definite phases, but the phases are by no means inevitable, nor do they occur in identical form among various societies. The emphasis upon self-determination in this study makes it clear that the great-man thesis is not entirely repudiated. Yet, the arguments are certainly not based on such a thesis. The theory is a representation of what might be termed a "little great-man thesis." Such a thesis means that every middle class individualist exercises some influence upon the development of the society in which he lives.

Democracy Defined

At this point a definition and discussion of democracy become pertinent to the general argument. Democracy is literally rule by the many, that is, self-rule. Ideally, democracy involves direct representation; but the mechanical problems arising from size of populations and geographic dispersion have brought about the development of democracy by indirect representation. The indirection of control has presented many new problems which modern political conveyances have not fully resolved. The problems may be divided into three broad categories, namely, those connected with responsibility of representatives to the electorate, those connected with responsibility of administrators to the representatives, and, most important, those connected with responsibility of constituents to their society.

Because this study is not primarily concerned with political conveyances and loyalties, the first two categories will not be discussed. The third category is important, however, in a study of the middle class. It is my personal opinion that the indirection of democratic controls has helped to bring about a form of unrestrained individualism bordering upon licentiousness. Individual members of modern democracies are disposed often to regard their liberty as a right for which they need make no payment. One point which cannot be overemphasized is the fact that there are no free rights in any aspect of human society. Freedom is a trust which must be honored at all times. Failure to honor the trust results inevitably in the loss of the freedom. In other words, responsibility is the price of freedom—and the price is payable in installments which never cease. Because the contributions of individuals in a society toward the maintenance of the trust are atomistic, the individual members may lose sight of the fact that such contributions are nevertheless fundamental. Unprincipled and unscrupulous demagogues do not hold public office where individual members of a society are assuming their democratic responsibilities. From the foregoing it is evident that unrestrained middle class development can be quite as damaging to a society as undue restraint. This problem was mentioned briefly in connection with Carthage and Phoenicia and will be discussed later when we come to the American culture.

Forms of Privilege

Closely related to the responsibilities which are inevitably connected with rights come the responsibilities which go with privilege. Insofar as the society as a whole is concerned, a special privilege extended to an individual or group must be justified upon the basis of a special contribution which that individual or group is making to the society. For example, one sees justification in frequent brief holidays for the executive head of a nation. The cost to the nation is infinitesimal in comparison with the value received in the form of more efficient executive direction. A transit company requires a franchise in order to effect the savings which normally accrue to a natural monopoly. But such a company is responsible for efficient internal management, and is expected to pass the resultant savings to the society in the form of lower rates. The feudal barons obtained the special privilege of overlordship, but in payment for this privilege they were responsible for the maintenance of peace and order within their territories.

Three serious problems arise in connection with privilege. First, the original social contract may be unfavorable to the society. The privilege is granted under terms whereby the individual or group receives special treatment but is not required to reciprocate by making a special contribution. From the beginning the society is the loser. The grant of certain rights or a monopoly to a courtier by an absolute monarch is a typical example. Second, a privilege may be granted on fair terms, but the recipient of the privilege may use the new power either to abrogate his obligations or else to seize more privilege than was originally implied. Third, the contract may be desirable at the time it is consummated, but as conditions alter with the passage of time the privilege may be retained long after the initial responsibility becomes meaningless. The retention of feudal rights is an example. On the other hand, new responsibilities may be shouldered by the privileged individual or group, in which event a new contract has, in essence, been established. The British system of constitutional monarchy is an example.

Privileges which are retained and which are not socially justified, or for which the justification has ceased to exist, must eventually pass from the holder. The absentee landlord cannot forever continue to hold his property rights. But, unfortunately for the society, institutional factors may operate to support the privilege for a long time—long enough to cause serious and even irreparable damage to the society itself. Holders of unjustified privileges are quite like parasites, and parasites can destroy the host upon which they fatten. Historical analysis would appear to indicate that the breakdown and disintegration of all societies to date have been accompanied by a compounding of parasitical privileges and restrictions.

The argument is here advanced that parasitical privileges and consequent restrictions constitute prime causal factors in the demise of civilizations. Parasitical privileges hamper the development of new or improved conveyances, and bring about a deterioration of existing conveyances. They also set up false local loyalties which interfere seriously with the healthy local loyalties, and also with the maintenance and expansion of the broader loyalties.

Institutions provide the form and strength whereby order is maintained in a society. They are essential for the creation and maintenance of a societal organization within which the conveyances and loyalties can operate. We shall not trouble ourselves here with the point that conveyances and loyalties are themselves institutional in form. The important feature is that institutions provide the means whereby the parasitical privileges and restrictions become established in the society, and later provide the defense whereby these privileges can resist extirpation. Institutional flexibility provides the means by which the parasitical privileges can be exposed and removed. Because institutional forms are less firmly established in the earlier stages of a society, the new society is better able to cleanse itself periodically of the parasitical encumbrances. Also, where middle class individualism develops, changes and adjustments in the institutional structure are frequent enough to help in the removal of the unwarranted privileges. As the institutions become more firmly established and more rigid, however, privilege and restriction begin to flourish. The generation of improved conveyances to match the broader loyalties is hampered. Societal deterioration sets in.

The institutional rigidities now operate for a lengthy period as sustaining factors. The structural strength which they provide helps to perpetuate the *status quo*. Internal disruptions, which may occur from time to time as the deterioration process continues, are resolved by more institutional restraints, until finally the civilization staggers from crisis to crisis and in the end collapses.

When the civilization does disintegrate, the conveyances break down, the broader loyalties are dissipated, and even the local loyalties are threatened, for they, too, are, in many instances, distorted and rotten with parasitical privileges. Individuals living in a collapsing civilization are lost. The privileged ones who no longer have their privileges and the burdened ones who formerly supported the privileges are both exposed to the rigors of disorganization, disruption, and chaos. And out of the maelstrom certain fundamental conveyances and loyalties emerge cleansed and rejuvenated. The successor civilization, geographically and biologically shifted, comes into existence.

CHAPTER NINE

The Theory Applied

———————◆———————

The fundamental problem in Western culture is the widening of the cultural lags. Abstractions based on physical realities are more easily comprehended than abstractions based upon human relationships. Human relationships could be termed mental or operational realities. Developments in the natural sciences have proceeded at a more rapid pace than developments in the social sciences, thus broadening the first cultural lag. As a result, a strong materialistic bias is evident in Western culture. This accent on materialism is particularly predominant in the American version of Western civilization.

The second cultural lag, that between intellectual leaders and the general populace, is especially important in democratic states. Under democracy the cohesive elements are maintained to a great extent by universal support. This dependence upon the general populace for active support means that improved comprehension and self-restraint by all of the citizens are necessary conditions for a healthy culture. The Greeks experimented with a democracy of intellectuals; Western civilization is experimenting with universal democracy. The attempt is courageous, but the challenges which Western society must face are thereby multiplied. If the experiment is to be successful, the cultural gap between the intellectual leaders and the general populace must be narrowed.

Western Europe

According to the terms of the analysis provided in the foregoing chapters, the present position of Western European states is fairly evident. They appear now to be approaching the end of their middle class activity, and are moving toward what is likely to be a lengthy period of staticism and universality. In material terms these states seem to have passed the apex of their greatness. But physical grandeur is often the prelude to cultural expansion and growth. The Western European states are now turning from materialism toward an appreciation of abstractions based on human relationships. Their culture is broadening and maturing.

But every culture must be prepared at all times to meet the threat of external force. The crucial problem which the Western European states face today is whether or not they can unite voluntarily to form a strong military and governmental unit. If so, Western Europeans may be able to escape the fate of the Greeks who suffered conquest at a similar period in their civilization. If the Western Europeans should unite, they may be able to enjoy the fruits of their culture with full sovereignty. Otherwise their future is likely to be clouded.

Specifically, England, the Netherlands, and the Scandinavian countries seem to have developed the most balanced societies in the group. The economic imbalance in France and Italy is a serious factor, although in many other fields of social activity these countries have a rich heritage. Germany affords an example of arrested development. There the middle class activity has early given way to a rigid military spirit wherein the individual is subjugated for the glory of the state. The progression of the German culture bears a striking resemblance in some respects to the reversion of the Spartan culture at an early stage in its development.

Russia is, of course, much behind the others in its development. That is why Russia constitutes the military threat for the Western European states. Russia appears at present to be passing through the age of tyrants. The great question is whether Russia will successfully negotiate this critical phase and proceed to a full-fledged development of a middle class, or whether, as in military states of the past, the progress will be arrested. The age of tyranny is yet too newly established for a satisfactory assessment, although the deliberate centralization of political, religious, and economic loyalties under the present tyranny may easily interfere with a proper middle class development. It is notable that the Greeks and English passed through their ages of tyranny in about one hundred and fifty years. We may therefore take this length of time as normal for a successful negotiation of this critical phase.[1]

For the current generation the conveyance of force probably offers the greatest challenge of all. Through productive effort, and this could occur through the economic leadership of the United States in particular, it may be possible for the Western European democracies to assert and to hold military supremacy in Europe. But the position of the European democracies today bears a startling resemblance to that of the Greek city-states in the third century B.C. The Hellenic culture was not destroyed through the failure of the Greek city-states to unite, but the Greeks lost their leadership to Rome because of this failure, and consequently lived out their period of universality in slavery instead of with sovereign freedom.

It would be easy to compare modern Germany to Sparta, the

[1] Some of my colleagues, who kindly read portions of this study in its draft form, indicated an interest in the application of these generalizations to the Oriental cultures. The generalizations in their present form are not applicable. The Oriental societal progressions have taken a somewhat different turn. Because a subjective interpretation of the Oriental mind would differ from that of the Occidental mind, a somewhat different theory would be required for a proper assessment of Oriental cultures. Therefore, the theory of the middle class as it has been developed is limited in its application to the Occidental world.

English-speaking peoples to the Athenians, and thus on in increasing detail. Yet, the analogy would certainly be strained if carried very far. Nevertheless, at the present time the Western democracies do face a distinct challenge. Are their conveyances efficient and powerful enough to help in building up the strong broader loyalties needed to meet the challenge? Sole reliance upon productive efficiency may easily prove inadequate. After all, in the beginning Rome was weaker than some of the unitary Greek states. The Romans merely took advantage of Greek disunity to play off one Greek state against another until they were so exhausted that domination over all of them became possible. The democracies of the Western culture could prove susceptible to such a device if their conveyances should prove to be inadequate to support the necessary broader loyalties in time to meet the challenge.

The Holy Alliance, the League of Nations, and the United Nations represent successive attempts to meet the challenge, but the almost complete reliance which these organizations have been compelled to place upon benevolence, voluntary cooperation, and vaguely conceived broader loyalties indicates a basic weakness. (Unity is not obtained through appeals to the finer emotions only. Real response depends upon the development of conveyances which arouse pride in and respect for the power of the unitary authority. Perhaps less vague idealism and more shrewd middle class thinking is needed in the conduct of international affairs among the Western democracies if a truly cohesive and well-integrated unitary authority is to be established. Failure to unite voluntarily could well mean the ultimate loss of freedom to an even more repressive authority.)

The development of backward areas in the world is another great challenge. Efforts of the United Nations and assistance of the United States in the form of capital goods and technical training are basic. Yet such assistance may easily become sterile unless the sociological aspects of the problem are fully explored. In addition to capital and technical know-how, these backward societies must be encouraged and helped in the development of a healthy and aggressive middle class if the progressive spirit is to be sparked and if the true democratic tradition is to spread.

The Cultural Lags in America

The American culture is somewhat less advanced in its development than the European. Middle class activity is still a potent force. Natural scientific and technological attainments are continuing at a phenomenal rate. There is, however, some evidence of a change in the pattern of growth. Individualistic and hence highly original achievements in the natural sciences are giving way to group research where originality is under some restraint. In the economic sphere, as John R. Commons noted, competitive capitalism has given way to financial capitalism, and now there are indications that the trend toward administrative capitalism is under way. The beginning of the end of the American industrial revolution is in sight. Atomic power may well mark the culmination.

Because of the phenomenal advances in the material aspects of the culture, and because the experiment of universal democracy[2] is being attempted in a most sweeping manner, the widening of the cultural lags is of particular significance. Social scientific progress has lagged pathetically behind the natural scientific attainments. As a result, an extreme emphasis upon materialism is now manifest in every aspect of the culture. In America, abstractions based upon the highly complex mental and operational realities are not adequately conceived even by the intellectual leaders. The social problems brought about by the physical innovations have proceeded too fast for the intellectual leaders to assimilate. That is the first cultural lag.

The second, that is, the lag between the intellectual leaders

[2] The American democracy is not truly universal in its ideals. A universal democracy would mean equal political, social, and economic opportunities and treatment.

and the general populace, is especially important because the sweeping democratic interpretation has given rise to the development of individual liberty on a scale which has no parallel in history. The cohesion of the society is now dependent to a large degree upon the mental perception and self-discipline of the individual members. For the ambitious American experiment to succeed, it is not sufficient for the intellectual leaders to close the cultural gap between the natural and social sciences. The gap between the intellectual leaders and the general populace must also be narrowed substantially. The responsibility of the leaders in helping to achieve this end may not be regarded lightly.

The Role of Privilege

In order to understand the problems involved in closing the cultural gaps, it is necessary to consider the ubiquitous influence which privilege has upon the human mind. Because the predatory nature of man makes privilege completely universal among human beings, all interrelationships of man with nature and more particularly of man with man are founded upon certain implicit or explicit assumptions concerning proper forms of privilege. The rights of private property, of inheritance, of a religious dogma, of a public official, of a host, of a guest—all are set out by regulation or custom in a given society. Each member of a social group enjoys a number of privileges which may be tacitly understood or explicitly stated, and owes to the group a number of obligations whereby the privileges of others are maintained. A just distribution of privileges and obligations depends upon the physical environment and the level of culture to which the group has attained. But with rare exceptions, such as the Hindu regard for lower forms of life, man's attitude toward nonhuman forms is purely exploitive. Animals are hunted, nurtured, or bred to provide some form of human satisfaction. Inanimate objects are altered for the same purpose. In all such relationships between man and nature the human viewpoint is paramount. The physical environment is made to conform to human desires as closely as the existing state of the arts permits.

Since there is little or no fundamental disagreement among members of the human species concerning the exploitive attitude toward nonhuman forms, the disagreements in this arena hinge upon two factors. The first is the method for its accomplishment. The second cause for disagreement is the effect which an alteration in the method might have upon existing social privileges.

Anthropomorphic man had the exploitive viewpoint, but because he lacked an objective perception he often attributed a personality to the nonhuman forms. He individualized them. Even modern man is not entirely objective toward inanimate objects. We speak of a ship as "she," and attribute a personality to it. The owner of an automobile or of a house becomes accustomed gradually to certain of its individual characteristics or peculiarities and begins to regard them much as one would regard the idiosyncrasies of a human being. He has individualized the object, and no longer views it in an entirely objective manner.

The process of generalization is a process of abstraction. The characteristic essentials are isolated and classified so that the phenomena may be reduced to a more simple and orderly pattern. But the generalizing process performs another and equally important function. It leads to an intellectual, dispassionate, and more completely objective viewpoint. Man easily develops an emotional attachment for a given object, such as a ship or a house or a car. Yet he dispassionately views the merits and demerits of this or that type of ship or house or car. His attitude toward nonhuman forms of life is similar, although emotional attachment may in this instance proceed to a further degree. One does not ordinarily develop an emotional attachment for houses in general, but it is quite possible to have an emotional regard for cats or for dogs in general.

Because the exploitive viewpoint toward all nonhuman forms is very nearly universal, and because improved techniques for generalization promote a dispassionate and objective viewpoint, the development of the natural sciences might easily have been clear cut and straightforward had it not been for the second form of disagreement among members of the human species. The desire to maintain given forms of social privilege manifests itself in all types of human society in the guise of vested interests. The inevitable result has been a multitude of prejudiced viewpoints, accompanied by local loyalties. The struggle for an objective viewpoint in the natural sciences has consequently been complicated, and in numerous instances advances have been retarded for considerable periods of time. But the barriers to natural scientific progress have been partial, or at best limited in duration. As we shall note shortly, societies have existed for long periods during which men were carefully taught to accept and to uphold the existing social privileges. This type of training is so common it might almost be termed the normal form. And yet, during periods when the dynamic factors are influential, no particular vested interest is strong enough to stop the advances of natural science. Even the most powerful form of church doctrine could not entirely stifle the scientific knowledge let loose by a Galileo.

When man reaches the stage where he can generalize and think objectively in a given area of natural scientific endeavor, the existing forms of social privilege must certainly, if grudgingly, give way and accommodate themselves to the new knowledge. In each case the knowledge thus obtained provides the means whereby man can exploit his physical environment more successfully. Natural scientific progress provides a greater opportunity for all members of the human species when the species is viewed collectively. The new forms of exploitation are primarily at the expense of nonhuman types. The greater command which the human species obtains over natural forces means, therefore, that the privileged position of man in general is enhanced.

But the improved knowledge concerning nonhuman phenomena does not mean that the position of individual men or groups of men is any better. To understand the conditions of life for individuals or groups of individuals we must consider the system of exploitation and of social privilege which exists in the particular human society under scrutiny. Man as an individual carries over from his contacts with nonhuman forms to his contacts with other human beings the same predatory or exploitive viewpoint. The small child does not distinguish between exploitation of his parents or playmates and exploitation of nonhuman forms. He seeks only to satisfy personal desires. When the cat objects to being mauled and scratches in retaliation, he learns to respect its powers in the same way that he respects the powers of a hot stove or the authority of a parent.

Only through training does he come to understand that exploitation of nonhuman forms is correct, but must be done in conformity with known physical forces for maximum satisfaction. Exploitation of fellow human beings, on the other hand, must be much more circumspect. Reason usually plays a very insignificant part in social training. The child is taught largely on an ethical basis. That is, he may be taught that exploitation of certain types of individuals or groups in a prescribed manner is correct, whereas a similar attitude toward other types of individuals or groups is incorrect. He may be taught that he has certain obligations to perform and that there are certain privileges he may enjoy. Because very little reason is attached to this mode of training, there need not be a logical balance between the rights and obligations. If the social class in which he is reared has a preferred status, the child quickly learns to accept and to claim as a right the preponderance of privileges he may enjoy in relation to the obligations he must fulfill. If, on the other hand, he is born into a slave class, he is just as quickly taught to accept the heavy load of obligations which are his lot. Regardless of his social status, he comes to understand that certain actions are improper. Rewards in the form of various satisfactions become associated with the first, and punishments in the form of various dissatisfactions become associated with the second. Once this pattern of thought and of behavior is fully established the child is socially adjusted, and normally will show emotional attachment for the established mode of behavior. The emotional attachment will occur regardless of whether the social status of the child is favorable or unfavorable. Only drastic alterations in the physical or social environments are likely to bring about a behavior change.

That is ethical training. Historically it has been the most common form. It is favored particularly in a class or caste society, for training of this sort helps to maintain the existing forms of privilege. It leads, of course, to social staticism.

A second type of training is more in evidence within a dynamic society. It is usually defined as the pragmatic type. The child learns from experience that the stove is hot, but also comes to realize from experience that it is useful. His problem is to find a way to use the heat without being burned. As he gains experience he learns to adopt this attitude toward all phenomena, natural or social. He is not inhibited by ethical training, and, therefore, he does not accept any particular form of natural or social exploitation as correct simply because it is customary. In order to gain his ends, which are purely predatory, he finds that he must analyze and reduce each problem to its essentials. In other words, he learns to be objective. He generalizes and abstracts universal knowledge which he can then use for intelligent exploitation.

This type of training is particularly productive insofar as the natural sciences are concerned. Social restrictions are at a minimum, and the exploitation of natural phenomena proceeds apace. So long as the predatory instinct is channeled into exploitation of nonhuman forms, such a society will favor freedom for the individual.

But, because the ethical form of training is not stressed, the child does not necessarily distinguish between exploitation of nonhuman forms and exploitation of human forms. He concentrates upon the first merely because it is more productive. When conditions are favorable he may therefore seek to exploit other human beings quite as readily and in the same way that he has been exploiting the nonhuman forms. When this occurs he becomes a ready disciple for such studies as Dale Carnegie's *How to Win*

Friends and Influence People. He is not an upholder of privilege but rather a seeker after privilege. Loyalty to the *status quo,* that is, to the existing social structure, takes second place to personal advancement. Such a child, if he is highly intelligent, becomes an innovator. This type of person is truly an individualist, a member of the middle class. If his activities are directed toward non-human forms he becomes a successful exploiter of the natural sciences. But, inasmuch as his energies are directed toward human relationships, he becomes an exploiter of mankind. Initially he may break down old and outmoded traditions and privileges, it is true, but only in order to erect new ones more favorable to himself. During the period of attack on the outmoded forms the individualist serves an extremely useful function, for he builds up a spirit of competition and of individual activity and a tradition of freedom. Thus he helps the society to emerge to a higher level of culture. An era of freedom for the individual ensues in which social privilege is reduced to a minimum, and the improvements resulting from a better system of exploitation of nonhuman forms are shared more equally.

But a dynamic society of this kind is highly unstable. The predatory and exploitive viewpoint is still paramount. Moreover, for the duller majority, freedom of this sort is dangerous. Ethical restraints are lacking, and there is a dearth of loyalties to which the nonthinking, nonreasoning majority can cling. Meanwhile the successful individualists find it profitable to cease the competition among themselves. By amalgamating they gain in two ways. First, they consolidate the privileged positions to which they have attained. And, second, they are better able as a group to exploit the majority. As a consequence they become less interested in exploitation of nonhuman forms and more interested in the exploitation of human beings outside their class.

Such a society is ripe for the demagogue. Because there is no clear delineation between privileges and obligations, the great majority come to feel insecure and lost in the social maelstrom. The path to freedom through the deliberate use of reason and intelligence is too arduous for them. In spite of their improved material position, they long for the shelter which despotic leadership provides. With both the successful individualists and the majority of the same opinion, although for different reasons, the tradition of freedom inevitably fades out.

New privileges, traditions, and restraints form. If the leadership is enlightened, the society integrates and stabilizes at a relatively high level of culture. But in any case, the opportunities for development of logical forms of thought and for the emergence of new knowledge become restricted. Knowledge becomes once again the private preserve of the select intelligentsia. Even these select few are encouraged to perpetuate existing forms of knowledge as a special privilege rather than to develop new knowledge. The era of pragmatism, of innovation, and of change then passes into an era of staticism, wherein proven formulas for handling physical phenomena and human relationships are followed blindly with little or no thought for the reason thereof. To question the formula in any instance becomes a sacrilegious act. Class privilege reigns supreme, and a period of ritual and tradition is re-enacted.

There is a third form of training, but few have trodden the path to which it leads. The Greeks found the way, and isolated individuals have since discovered it; but never since the Greek era has it been a way of life for a whole society. Suppose we try to see just how it differs from the two forms of training already described.

The fundamental factor is the disregard for privilege in any form—not only for the privilege of others but also for the privilege of self. The viewpoint is simply not exploitive. The child learns that the fire is hot, but he is also taught not to fear it on that account. Fire is the great Promethean gift to man, something to enjoy. It is a source of happiness. The green woods, the mountains, the cool waters of the Aegean Sea—all are gifts which nature has bestowed upon man. They are things to be used, not in a spirit of exploitation, but in a spirit of happiness, as one would

enjoy any gift freely given and freely accepted. Similarly knowledge is not something to be gathered in fear of transgression.
Holders of existing knowledge are not privileged individuals with
vested interests which may not be disturbed. They give freely of
their store. Knowledge is free. It is a gift to be had for the asking.
True, the seeker after knowledge must bestir himself, for he is
engaging in the most arduous activity of all, mental effort. Yet he
soon finds that the pleasure is as much in the chase as in the cap-
ture. The knowledge is not something which one gains for an
ulterior motive, as when the pragmatist seeks knowledge in order
to attain some form of privilege over man or nature; rather, it is
something to be valued for itself. Beauty and happiness and
symmetry are everywhere. The challenge is to seek them out and
to appreciate them. The desire for privilege is channeled into a
competitive spirit, wherein each contestant seeks to show by
sheer excellence of attainment that he truly appreciates the
great gifts which nature has bestowed upon him. Physical culture,
sculpture, music, oratory, poetry, drama, philosophy are all part
of the rounded and balanced life where the individual in complete
freedom of expression seeks to enjoy, and in doing so learns to
appreciate, the magnificent gifts which nature has showered upon
man.

A society with a religion, but without fear; with an effective
government, but free of restraint; with the knowledge to use the
gifts which nature provides so profusely, but cleansed of the
contaminating spirit of exploitation; filled with a desire to be active in all aspects of human endeavor, but not motivated by ulterior aims of privilege—can such a society ever recur in the history of man? In a small area and for a select few it did occur for a
brief period of time. Perhaps with intelligent effort the conditions
for a recurrence on a larger scale, on a more elevated level, and
on a more permanent basis can be brought into existence. The
first step in such a momentous undertaking is to understand precisely what the necessary conditions are. To accomplish this purpose we must certainly remove the rose-colored spectacles which

we are accustomed to using when we view the human species.

The three forms of training provide the clue to a proper development of culture. The ethical form, through its emphasis upon conformity, is emotional and nonreasoning in character. Group loyalties are deliberately cultured to maintain societal cohesion. The ethical system provides stability and ensures adherence to the socially accepted traditions. It does not ensure the best possible responses to the environmental challenges. An ethical system which does not conform well enough to the challenges to bring about societal survival cannot endure, of course. Either the system is modified or the society perishes. In either case that particular system eventually disappears, although it may last a long time if the total culture is well advanced above subsistence level.

The pragmatic system of training is particularly effective in relationships with nonhuman forms, whether animate or inanimate. Moreover, it is also a means whereby outmoded customs and traditions may be altered to meet new conditions. But pragmatism does not deal adequately with the pernicious forms of privilege. The spirit of exploitation continues to predominate. So long as the exploitive activity is directed to nonhuman forms, the viewpoint is reasonably objective and a scientific approach is possible. Consequently, pragmatism is admirably suited to the natural sciences. Again, so long as there is an active group of middle class individualists who are seeking to improve their position in the social hierarchy, outmoded social privileges based upon ethical acceptance will be challenged and modified with reasonable speed. But, as these middle class individualists move into the upper class, their undoubtedly superior intelligence and activity are directed toward maintenance of the *status quo*. They thus form a powerful reinforcement for the upholders of privilege. New middle class individualists then find it increasingly difficult to maintain the newborn tradition of social dynamics. The progressive period then inevitably passes, and the society lapses slowly into staticism and eventual decay.

Unfortunately, historical studies indicate that the static periods greatly exceed the dynamic periods in length of time. We are exceedingly fortunate to live in one of the brief dynamic periods. Yet, even now, there is increasing evidence in all forms of social relationships that the current period of individual freedom and progress may be drawing to an end, that is, we may be approaching another long period of social staticism, commonly known as a period of universality.

Determinism vs. Self-Determination

Inasmuch as social dynamics and social statics are man-made phenomena, it is logical to assume that they are amenable to deliberately planned modification. In other words, if we assume that social progress and social stagnation are purely the result of human attitudes, it is reasonable to conclude that we can exercise some measure of control over these societal phases.

First, suppose we examine the basic assumption. The human species, like all forms of life, is certainly influenced by physical environment. The Egyptian culture was largely the product of the Nile River, just as the Mesopotamian culture was the product of the Tigris and Euphrates, and the Hindu culture the product of the Indus. The Phoenicians and the Greeks, and, later, the Romans were profoundly influenced by the Mediterranean. In more recent times the Western European culture was developed largely as a result of relatively easy inland navigation and the invitation of the Atlantic. Geographic determinism is not an argument to be dismissed lightly. Physical environment unquestionably does exercise a profound influence upon human activities and upon social relationships.

But geographic determinism in itself provides an inadequate explanation for human development. Different peoples at similar periods or even the same people at different periods react quite individually to identical physical challenges: factors other than physical environment must also influence human activities. It might be correct to say that the physical environment sets the framework within which human activities take place. Since, however, the human species is showing rather remarkable talent in modifying the physical environment, it might even be said that the framework itself is subject to at least some modification. In any case, there is a sufficient measure of freedom in connection with physical environment for the human species to exercise at least some control over its own societal phases.

The other limitation upon freedom of choice and of action by the human species is more difficult to assess, and consequently the measure of freedom which may be left is more conjectural. This limitation is the one imposed by the physical, intellectual, and emotional characteristics of the human species itself. A proper assessment of this limitation would, of course, entail a most exhaustive study and appraisal of the species, and the question naturally arises whether man as a member of the human species could possibly appraise his own genus accurately. The only answer to such a question is that man is the sole choice for such a task. Either we throw up our hands in despair, or we simply do the best we can. In the latter event there can be no apologies. By our very actions we are assuming that our own physical, intellectual, and emotional limitations are not so all-pervasive that we cannot exercise at least some freedom in determining the future course of our own species. Once this point is clearly understood it will no longer seem strange to hear a social scientist speaking of the human species as if it were a type of animal with which he is not personally connected. After all, we are quite accustomed to speech of this sort by physicians when they speak of the human body.

If, then, the assumption that societal relationships are man-made and therefore man-controlled, in part at least, is acceptable, we may now pass on to the problem of how the control may be exerted. In this connection recognition of the role which privilege plays is fundamental. So long as the exploitive attitude is accepted without question or discrimination, an alternation of ethical and pragmatic periods in the development of man becomes the normal and, one might reasonably say, the inevitable form. Since the pragmatic viewpoint is particularly effective in the natural sciences, would it be possible to encourage an exploitive attitude toward all nonhuman forms and at the same time adopt a nonexploitive viewpoint toward social relationships? After all, the Greeks did something of this sort when they built their culture upon a system of slave economics. They simply drew the line beyond rather than at the demarcation between the human and nonhuman forms. Slaves were relegated to the nonhuman group. Yet it might be said that the ultimate breakdown and reversion of their culture to the ethical form was brought about largely by this conflict. Actually, such a picture is not truly accurate. The Greeks accepted slavery as a normal societal condition, but evidence would indicate that they exploited their slaves less than had the older cultures. The general Hellenic viewpoint was nonexploitive within a given framework of custom and tradition. The greatness of the Greek culture lay in the nonexploitive viewpoint; and this was reinforced by the relative, though not absolute, tolerance toward the outsider.

To say that the human species may not be predatory would be to deny the right of survival. All forms of animal life must use other living matter in one way or another. But there is a difference between using and exploiting. A society which concentrates upon using its environment is not heavily encumbered by restrictive traditions of privilege. Such a society is ever alert to possible improvements in the manner of use. Its level of culture is limited by the level of the abstractions to which it has attained, but the way to improvement is ever open. The challenge to the human mind is clear and immediate. Such a society is necessarily dynamic.

The exploitive society, on the contrary, by its collective viewpoint encourages the growth of privilege. Individuals and, more particularly where social relationships are concerned, groups of individuals seek always to gain advantage. During the pragmatic phase the exploitation is directed toward nonhuman forms. But, so long as the exploitive viewpoint is present, the exploitation of human forms inevitably follows. Once relative advantages over other human beings are gained, the dominant groups expend their efforts in maintaining their privileges. These privileges are soon claimed as rights and defended as such. The exploitive society therefore soon turns its attention to relative advantages for special groups; consequently the absolute advantages which would accrue from improvements in physical and social environment are neglected, and often vehemently opposed lest such changes endanger the existing social privileges.

The Future of America

The alternative paths along which the American society may move can now be examined. Unfortunately, in view of the characteristically exploitive attitude of the culture—and what is worse, in view of the many pernicious forms of privilege which appear to be developing[3]—the two most evident paths are not pleasant to contemplate.

One possibility is that the cultural gaps may widen to the extent that leadership assumes the form of military repression and state glorification. Such a possibility is always present in any society, but in the current instance it may be more than ordinarily significant. External threats to the safety of the state invariably raise the prestige of the military leaders and render possible a military *coup d'état*. There are the examples of Sparta and Germany. Rome also came under the power of the military dur-

[3] Lobby groups, self-seeking politicians, professional bureaucrats, utility interests, restrictive monopolists in which some professional groups may be included, labor unions, special agricultural interests, are all operating openly and insidiously to advance their special interests on a scale that has no parallel throughout the civilized world. Nor is the system of checks and compromises working necessarily in the public interest. More often it is a case of deals or bargains at public expense—a system of "You scratch my back and I'll scratch yours, and the public be damned." This was largely the position of Carthage prior to its fall. No society can endure when the parasitic forms of privilege reach such proportions that the broader loyalties no longer predominate.

ing the imperial period of her history. We are too well acquainted with modern fascist movements in some of the European and Latin-American countries to be unaware of this ever-present danger. Military leaders do not attempt to solve the societal problems through intellectual leadership. They choose rather to use the more direct and simple device of forcible repression. Cultural development is frozen; individualism and all forms of original thinking are stifled. The cultural lags are closed by regression instead of advancement. The price paid for the restoration of cohesion in the society is high, since the culture becomes sterile and static.

The second possibility is the Carthaginian form. In the event that this development should occur we might expect to see a continuation of the growth of pernicious forms of privilege in the society. Restrictive monopolistic forces, under cover of a barrage of propaganda to the effect that they are really competitive,[4] might eventually assume real control of the state, probably by amalgamating forces with the military. In doing so the restrictive monopolists would undoubtedly claim to be saving the society from some evil force. The present threat is communism, but it could be any force which is highly disturbing to the great majority and which represents chaos in the minds of the people.[5] It

[4] Strangely enough, under conditions of pure competition there is little or no advertising. Extensive advertising is a sure sign of nonprice competition which is characteristic of oligopolistic and monopolistic conditions.

[5] Fear and hate are symptoms of ignorance. We understand machines and natural scientific processes. Therefore, we respect but do not fear certain physical dangers involved in their use. But, because we do not properly understand the abstractions involved in social relationships, we are confused and afraid. There are real dangers in international relationships, but we do not rationally distinguish between real dangers and imaginary ones. Consequently we are more likely to injure ourselves. America cannot run away from international relationships any more than an individual in contemporary society can run away from machines. Therefore, we must learn to understand the social abstractions involved in the international relationships. In that way the benefits which accrue from these relationships can be obtained, and at the same time the real dangers can be recognized and avoided. It is not necessary to give up internal liberties any more than it was necessary for primitive peoples to live in the shadow of superstitious fears. Mental effort to assimilate the abstractions involved in social relationships is the price of freedom today.

should be kept in mind that such control could be seized and held even while the legal forms of the Constitution were upheld to the letter. Incidentally, by posing as the saviors of democracy, the monopolistic forces would gain added prestige.

The essential point is that the translation of the second possibility into reality would mean that the American experiment had ended in failure. Rank materialism would continue to be the essential motivating factor in the society, and the society itself would be in the grip of the forces of privilege. This was the position into which Carthage had moved prior to its downfall. In such a situation the parasitic privileges and restrictions choke out the healthy aspects of the culture. The society has begun to feed on itself. The infamous China lobby provides a classic example of Carthaginian corruption. Through it the United States has lost prestige among its allies, and has become committed to a most unrealistic, if not disastrous, policy in the Far East.

The third possibility is somewhat more hopeful. In this case the intellectual leadership is so advanced that it has to impose its enlightened decisions with simple explanations only. The leaders would gladly explain the true situation, but because the general populace cannot comprehend reasonable arguments, the explanations provided by the leaders must be extremely elementary and must be backed by authority. The treatment of underdeveloped colonial peoples by the English is a modern example. Americans in some instances have adopted the same policy toward the Negro population. If the intellectual leadership is truly enlightened, these leaders will behave toward their followers in much the same manner as an affectionate but responsible parent behaves toward a child. The treatment is authoritative but humanitarian. Every effort is made to help the uncultured followers to gain understanding. Moreover, as they do progress, liberties and responsibilities are relinquished to them.

The fourth possibility is probably the highest practical objective in the present society. Here the society would have intellectual leadership of the highest form. The general populace would also have a balanced culture whereby through broad understanding its members would assume most liberties and responsibilities. They would, however, be sufficiently enlightened to appreciate the need for delegation of some authority to the intellectual leaders. In other words, they would know enough to comprehend the shortcomings in their own cultural development, and would recognize the existence of a definite, though probably narrow, cultural gap between themselves and the intellectual leaders. As a result, a completely harmonious society would exist in which there would be a broad measure of toleration, freedom, and self-discipline, accompanied by some societal restraints. The need for these restraints would be fully appreciated, and as a consequence they would be cheerfully accepted in the societal interest.

The fifth possibility is purely an ideal. In such a society both cultural lags would have been completely eliminated. Complete freedom and complete responsibility and self-restraint would make formal laws unnecessary. Proudhon's idyllic state of anarchy would become a reality. This fifth possibility pictures a condition which stirs the imagination, but an appreciation of it is probably important only because such contemplation inspires the highest form of effort.

Social Justice

This raises the age-old question concerning the meaning of justice. Plato supplied an excellent answer for his day, but is that answer adequate for the contemporary culture? Plato spoke of a society in which there would be men of brass to engage in trade and commerce, men of silver to protect the state, and men of gold to provide the political and cultural leadership. Plato recognized the need for intellectual leadership of a high caliber, and discussed at length the manner in which these leaders were to be selected and trained. Heredity was to play no part since parasitical privilege might thereby grow. He accepted the second cultural lag as inevitable. Consequently he did not view the democratic principle with favor. His concept of an operational form of justice was essentially static. It should be kept in mind that he was merely seeking some means whereby the given culture could be perpetuated, and was not concerned with further societal growth and development. For that reason he favored a small, compact state wherein the intellectual leaders would not have difficulty in keeping the first cultural lag closed.

If the concept of justice is broadened to include dynamic problems and if the ideal of universal democracy is to be considered, some modification of the Platonic conception is necessary. Suppose we consider the problem by accepting these rather rigid though implicit assumptions as a starting point. The assumptions can then be relaxed progressively.

Plato assumed a static society and accepted a permanent second cultural gap. His form of justice then operated to bring about a balanced and harmonious society under these conditions. Suppose the static assumption is removed. The intellectual leaders must then accept the continuous challenge presented by the growing complexities of societal life. General and specific mental conveyances must be constantly formulated and reformulated on an ever higher level so that the first cultural lag may not become a serious factor. But the basic form of the society does not need to change. There can still be men of brass, men of silver, and men of gold.

Suppose we now remove the second assumption, namely, the permanent second cultural lag. Suppose, first, that the lag exists, but that the democratic ideal is present. In this event the just society must take steps to close the second cultural lag in order that the democratic ideal may be attained. The society takes the form outlined under the third possibility, that is, one with a paternalistic leadership. As the second cultural lag is narrowed, the fourth and, ideally, the fifth possibilities may become relevant. In this event, both leaders and followers would progress toward equality at a high intellectual and ethical level.

According to this interpretation, justice becomes a relative quality. Justice exists when the degrees of freedom and the burdens of responsibility are apportioned according to the existing state of the cultural lags. Also, the just society seeks always to advance to higher levels of culture. Such advance must, however, always be geared to the rate at which the intellectual leaders can develop their perceptions. In this way the first cultural lag does not develop. Moreover, so that the democratic ideal may be attained, the second cultural gap must not broaden unduly. As long as these conditions exist, the society is always in balance.

If we apply this concept to the American society, its position becomes evident. With the formation of the republic the third or even the fourth possibilities were attempted. In the young republic the abstractions were not too complex and the intellectual leaders were therefore able to provide adequate leadership. Moreover, the abstractions could also be conceived in more elementary form by the general populace. Consequently, the democratic forms were possible without bringing about imbalance. But in the intervening period the situation has altered radically. Through growth and development brought about by the fermenting activities of the middle class many of the abstractions have become exceedingly complex. The first cultural lag, that between the natural sciences and the social sciences, or to put it another way, the lag in the development and comprehension by the intellectual leaders of adequate conveyances to sustain the ever broader loyalties, has widened to a serious extent. Also, in spite of the system of universal education, the mental lag between the intellectual leaders and the general populace is showing signs of widening. Unless the first gap is narrowed substantially the ultimate existence of the society is threatened; and unless the second gap is narrowed the tradition of democracy is jeopardized.

To rephrase in somewhat poetic similes, freedom is a delicate plant; cultivated and nurtured, it blossoms profusely, bearing strange and bountiful fruits in bewildering variety; assumed and neglected, it is soon choked out by ugly weeds of ignorance, intolerance, fear, and hate. No one can take freedom for granted, for it generates change and raises new problems even while it is bringing about improvements in the level of culture. We cannot continue to have the improvements in the culture unless we are willing to face the new complexities involved; either we desire freedom and progress and work unceasingly to maintain them, or we shrink from the mental effort involved and turn instead to the pseudo security of authoritarianism.

Appendix and Bibliography

Expansion of the Firm and Industry under Imperfect Competition[1]

The concept of a downward sloping demand curve, based on the law of diminishing marginal utility (or the diminishing marginal rate of substitution), the entry of new buyers as the price declines, and the almost universal tendency to substitute purchases toward a commodity as its price falls, is firmly established in economic analysis. The concept of an upward sloping supply curve, however, rests on a more questionable premise. Increasing average costs in the short run arising from factor indivisibilities or the law of nonproportional returns are normal. But in the long run, unless one or more of the fixed factors are fixed by nature or some other exogenous and immutable force, average costs may remain constant or may even decline over extraordinarily large ranges of production.

This situation is fully recognized with respect to the industry. Indeed, we often speak of increasing, constant, and decreasing

---

[1] This Appendix is designed to demonstrate through price analysis the contention contained in Chapter Seven that expansion may occur through growth of existing firms rather than through an increase in the number of firms.

cost industries. But economic theorists do not appear to have grasped the idea that the same conditions may apply to individual firms. A long-run increase in the rate of output for the industry is not necessarily or even ordinarily accomplished through an expansion in the number of firms. The existing firms may simply grow. Even without an increase in the rate of output for the industry, it is quite possible for some firms to expand at the expense of others.

In his article, "The Equilibrium of the Firm," Nicholas Kaldor argues that where indivisibility of factors exists, unit costs will fall for a time and then rise as the factors which are fixed in the short run become overused.[2] But as output is increased over the long run a succession of optimum points may be reached. Moreover, he maintains that there is no reason why the level of these optimum points should rise unless the industry as a whole is faced with increasing costs. It might be argued further that even where there are external diseconomies to bring about increasing costs for the industry, individual firms within the industry might still grow.

To restrain the growth of individual firms, internal diseconomies must operate through one or more fixed factors, but these factors must not be fixed for the industry. One such fixed factor for the firm might be the coordinating function of management. Yet, coordination is a dynamic function required for adjustments only, and consequently its limiting influence is questionable. Kaldor also examines the possible correlation between the age of a firm and its relative efficiency of operation. He finds that such a correlation is also highly questionable. He concludes, therefore, that, in the absence of other restraining influences, the technical optimum size of the firm is indeterminate.

In his article, "The Principle of Increasing Risk," M. Kalecki argues that the rising cost of capital as the firm goes into the loan market on a larger and larger scale is the internal diseconomy

[2] Nicholas Kaldor, "The Equilibrium of the Firm," *Economic Journal* (1934), pp. 60-76.

which limits the growth of the individual firm.[3] Such a limitation may be of some significance for very small firms operating under conditions of pure or almost pure competition. But a glance at the real world is sufficient to show that under conditions of imperfect competition large amounts of equity capital can be obtained through incorporation and sale of stock. Also, as the firm grows in size and prestige it is able to borrow in the loan market on not less favorable but rather on more favorable terms. Finally, expansion through the use of undistributed profits is currently practiced on an ever-increasing scale.[4]

In Chapter VII of *The Economics of Imperfect Competition* Joan Robinson speaks of normal profits, above which new firms will be encouraged to enter and below which existing firms may drop out. R. F. Harrod, in commenting on this point, notes that there may be a profit rate below that required to bring in new firms, yet high enough to encourage expansion by existing firms.[5] One might conceive such a profit rate as being of increasing significance as the market becomes more imperfect and as entry becomes more difficult. Finally, J. R. Hicks observes the disequilibrating forces for the firm on pages 85-88 of his *Value and Capital*, but does not attempt to pursue the subject.[6]

At this point we might recapitulate briefly. First, we have noted that, while long-run increasing costs for an industry will occur where there are external diseconomies, a great range of output at constant or decreasing costs is often possible. This possibility is highly significant in areas where mass production techniques are feasible. Second, factors which might restrain the growth of

[3] M. Kalecki, "The Principle of Increasing Risk," *Economica* (1937), pp. 440-447. See also the comment on this article by N. S. Buchanan and R. D. Calkins, and Kalecki's reply, *Economica* (1938), pp. 455-460.

[4] For the American economy undistributed profits in 1953 amounted to over $10 billions, or more than one third of net savings (Federal Reserve Bulletin).

[5] R. F. Harrod, "A Further Note on Decreasing Costs," *Economic Journal* (1933), pp. 337-338.

[6] J. R. Hicks, *Value and Capital* (London: Oxford University Press, 1939).

firms within an industry exercise a doubtful influence.[7] Moreover, for the firm operating under conditions of imperfect competition the disequilibrating forces are strengthened. With these points in mind we may now turn to equilibrium problems connected with oligopolies and monopolies.

In economic analysis it has become so customary to think of oligopolies and monopolies as organizations which restrict output and maintain exploitive prices that their expansive tendencies under given conditions have been largely neglected. It is true that where conditions do not favor expansion, oligopolies and monopolies will adopt a static viewpoint, and will restrict output so that they may exploit the market through relatively high prices. But with present mass production techniques the restrictive oligopolies and monopolies are exceptional. For most of them an expansive and progressive attitude is more advantageous. This is particularly true in the American market, where standardization and mass production techniques have been developed to an extreme degree.

In order to develop the above thesis, suppose we examine first the conditions under which restrictive oligopolies and monopolies operate. In Figure 1 the position of the restrictive oligopoly is illustrated, and in Figure 2 the restrictive monopoly. In both instances it is notable that average long-run costs beyond the point of equilibrium are increasing. Also, the demand for the industry is assumed fixed. Under these circumstances it definitely pays each firm to adopt a restrictive attitude and to maximize profits through exploitation of the given market. But in most instances neither of these conditions is realistic.

[7] Eli W. Clemens has suggested that this argument can be strengthened further. He points out that existing firms are disposed to expand output so long as there is any group which has a potential demand for the firm's product or other product which the firm can readily produce, provided the marginal cost of such additional output, including marginal selling costs, is less than the marginal revenue. Moreover, through product differentiation and price discrimination the market for the original output may be kept isolated. New firms, on the other hand, would require at least average costs to enter. See his article, "Price Discrimination and the Multiple Product Firm," *Review of Economic Studies* (1950-1951), pp. 1-11. I am grateful to Professor Clemens for a number of valuable comments and suggestions on this paper.

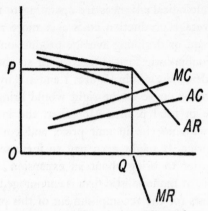

FIGURE 1A—Restrictive Oligopoly

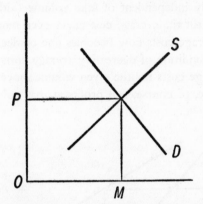

FIGURE 1B—Industry Graph of Restrictive Oligopoly
(Undifferentiated Product)

We may consider first the problem of average long-run costs. The majority of oligopolies and monopolies are in the manufacturing or other secondary industries, and it is in these industries especially that production on a massive scale brings about lower and lower unit production costs. A constant or declining average production cost curve would illustrate the conditions of operation more accurately. For the great majority of firms the stage of long-run increasing unit production costs has not been reached. Moreover, rapid technological advances are operating to make the stage of increasing average production costs ever more remote.

With constant or declining average production costs, the oligopolistic or monopolistic firm is faced with an entirely different situation from that indicated in Figures 1 and 2. Any movement of the average revenue curve to the right would bring about a substantial increase in total profits. Moreover, the increased profits would accrue with no rise in unit price, and could occur even with a fall in price. It might even pay to increase average costs somewhat in order to bring about an expansion of the market. The oligopolistic or monopolistic firm is encouraged to incur additional selling costs for the accomplishment of this purpose.

But the additional selling costs, being in the fixed cost category and largely independent of sales volume (although not vice versa), lift and tilt the average cost curve even more. A condition of constant average costs now becomes one of decreasing average costs, while a condition of decreasing average costs is accentuated. The total average costs for the given volume move up toward the average revenue, of course, and profits at that volume tend to be

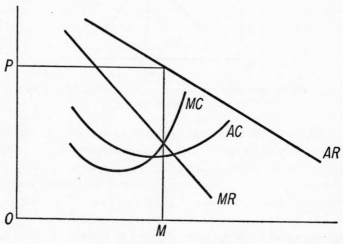

FIGURE 2—Restrictive Monopoly

eliminated. But the increased selling costs cause the demand for the product to grow. The average revenue curve moves to the right. The producer will normally obtain a smaller profit per unit sale, but may easily more than make up for this in increased volume.[8]

The new selling price for the product could be a little higher, although it is much more likely to be the same or lower, since an increase in selling price could militate against an increase in sales and might easily pyramid the selling costs. Graphically, if the increased unit selling costs more than offset the decrease in unit production costs, the selling price may move up, although not necessarily so; but if the increased unit selling costs are offset or more than offset by the decrease in unit production costs, the selling price will almost certainly be the same or lower. Figures 3 and 4 illustrate the industry expansion. They show the case where the price decreases as the volume grows.

Thus far we have concentrated on the problem of constant or decreasing average production costs. Actually, the ease or difficulty with which the oligopolist or monopolist can expand sales volume is crucial to the argument. In seeking to expand his sales the oligopolist or monopolist may use three different approaches. He may seek to open up new markets through geographic or extensive development of the market area. He may seek to broaden sales within the existing market area by educating buyers as to the desirability of the product or by developing new uses for the product. Finally, he may raid the markets of his competitors.[9]

---

[8] Some oligopolies, such as the steel companies or other capital goods companies which have very high fixed costs, may hesitate to expand freely even when they have decreasing average costs. The violent fluctuations in demand for their products arising from the business cycle may make such companies particularly fearful of excess plant capacity. Accelerated depreciation allowances can overcome this fear in some measure, but it is a factor to be considered.

[9] For the oligopolist the raiding may take the form of nonprice competition or expansion into multiproduct output. For the monopolist expansion into multiproduct output is the only means of raiding. This may make him in part an oligopolist. Multiproduct output raises the question of common

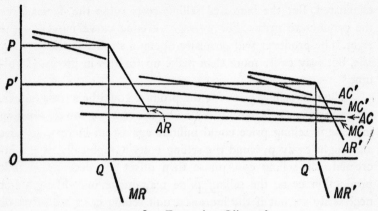

FIGURE 3A—Expansive Oligopoly

AC represents the original average cost. *AC'* represents the new average cost when added selling costs are included.

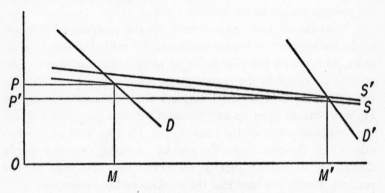

FIGURE 3B—Industry Graph of Expansive Oligopoly
(Undifferentiated Product)

Because the oligopolistic and monopolistic firms are concentrated for the most part in the secondary industries, they are especially favored. The demand for their products can be intensively developed with relative ease in comparison with the inelastic and

and separable costs, and brings up the further question of average costing procedures. Since this problem does not lend itself to graphical illustration, it is omitted from consideration.

rigid demand for agricultural products. Consequently, the sales expansion of manufactured items within the existing market has proceeded and is still proceeding at a phenomenal rate. This, again, is particularly true in the American economy. Many manufactured items which did not form part of the normal wants of the average individual in the society a generation ago have now become conventional needs. The educating process as to the desirability and uses of these products has proceeded apace and shows little sign of slackening even yet.

Also, the rapidity with which the oligopolistic and monopolistic firms have extended their operations throughout the national market indicates the ease with which geographic expansion can be carried out when there are no tariff or exchange barriers. In fact, a substantial proportion of these firms already operate on a nation-wide basis. The question now arises as to how much international expansion can possibly take place before the extensive limitations begin to operate. This depends in part upon political factors in the form of stability of foreign governments and the attitude of these foreign governments as manifested by their tariff policies, exchange controls, and treatment of outside investors. Inevitably, the attitude of the home government is also fundamental, since the attitude of foreign governments is often a reflection of or reaction to it.

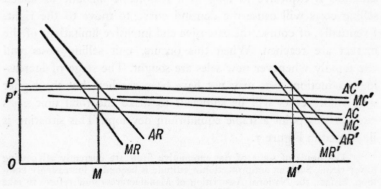

FIGURE 4—Expansive Monopoly

Some oligopolists and monopolists now operating on a nation-wide basis in the American economy appear to be dimly aware of their predicament.[10] To maintain their traditional policy of progress and expansion they must turn their attention to foreign markets. But, in order to expand sales in this fashion, they must be willing to back a free-trade policy and accept international competition in the home market. This is quite contrary to traditional thinking concerning trade barriers, and is a bitter pill to swallow. Thus we have two traditional modes of thought in conflict, and as yet unresolved.

The third technique for expanding sales, that is, by raiding markets of competitors through nonprice competition or by expanding into multiproduct output, is for the most part corrosive. Apart from the educating effect of the advertising, it does not bring about an increase in total demand for a particular product. It merely indicates the process whereby weaker oligopolies are eliminated or, more commonly, amalgamated.

It is interesting to note that the Cobweb Theorem helps to illustrate the expansive tendencies. The theorem itself is concerned with static equilibrium, but by allowing for shifts in the supply and demand curves the dynamic process can be indicated. In Figure 5 increasing costs encourage stability. Here the case of the restrictive oligopoly or monopoly would apply. But in Figure 6 the situation is explosive as long as a reasonable amount of added selling costs will cause the demand curve to move to the right. Eventually, of course, the extensive and intensive limitations of the market are reached. When this occurs, unit selling costs will rise rapidly whenever new sales are sought. The stage of increasing production costs may not have been reached, but the higher unit selling costs will be sufficient to make the total unit costs rise. At this point a stable equilibrium develops. This situation is illustrated in Figure 7.

[10] The heads of some of the automotive firms are currently advocating lower tariffs. Such an antiprotectionist attitude is becoming increasingly common. In fact, the National Association of Manufacturers now refuses to take a stand in the matter because of divergent opinions among the members.

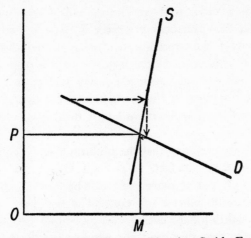

FIGURE 5—The Cobweb Theorem, Showing Stable Equilibrium

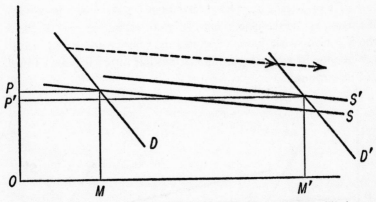

FIGURE 6—The Cobweb Theorem, Showing Unstable Equilibrium

Expansion continues as long as the selling costs incurred in moving the demand curve to the right do not cause total unit costs to rise.

In the present situation the intensive development of the market is continuing, but the intensive development alone may easily prove insufficient for continued economic development. In that probable event, unless there is also an extensive expansion whereby the oligopolists and monopolists give up their nationalistic privileges in order to move into the world market on a massive scale, we may reasonably expect a pulsating and gradual slowing down of the expansive tendencies as unit selling costs mount. If this should occur, the majority of the oligopolists and monopolists will become restrictive. They will cease to concentrate upon an expansion of the market either extensively or intensively, and will turn their attention to the exploitation of the given market.

It is well worth noting that the problem is not one of increasing production costs. In fact, technological advances continually make this problem ever more remote. The real problem is the threat of increasing unit selling costs. The national markets are becoming too small for the ever-growing oligopolistic and monopolistic firms. On the other hand, the political and ideological difficulties to be surmounted in bringing about the necessary expansion of world trade may be greater than we are prepared to face. If this should be the case, the great era of economic growth which the Western world has experienced may finally come to an end— not because of technological limitations but rather because of market limitations.

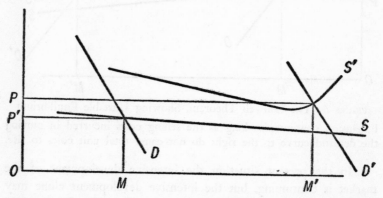

FIGURE 7—The Cobweb Theorem, with Stable Equilibrium Restored
This condition occurs when the demand curve becomes sufficiently resistant to further shifting to bring about a rapid rise in unit selling costs.

Selected Bibliography

BREASTED, JAMES HENRY

A History of Egypt. New York: Charles Scribner's Sons, 1912.
Ancient Times: A History of the Early World. Boston: Ginn & Co., 1914.
The Conquest of Civilization. New York: Harper & Brothers, 1926.

CHILDE, V. GORDON

Man Makes Himself. New York: New American Library, 1951.
The Bronze Age. New York: The Macmillan Company, 1930.
What Happened in History. Harmondsworth, England: Penguin Books, Ltd., 1942.

COMTE, AUGUSTE

Positive Philosophy. London: George Bell & Sons, Ltd., 1896.

DAVIS, KINGSLEY

Human Society. New York: The Macmillan Company, 1949.

DURANT, WILL

The Story of Philosophy. New York: Simon and Schuster, 1926.

DURKHEIM, ÉMILE

The Rules of the Sociological Method. Chicago: The University of Chicago Press, 1938.

The Elementary Forms of the Religious Life. New York: The Macmillan Company, 1926.

Suicide. Glencoe, Ill.: The Free Press, 1951.

ELLWOOD, CHARLES

A History of Social Philosophy. New York: Prentice-Hall, Inc., 1938.

FRAZER, JAMES GEORGE

The Golden Bough. New York: The Macmillan Company, 1940.

GROSECLOSE, ELGIN

Money: The Human Conflict. Norman: University of Oklahoma Press, 1934.

HANSEN, ALVIN H.

Business Cycles and National Income. New York: W. W. Norton & Company, 1951.

HOMER

The Iliad. New York: Modern Library, n.d.

The Odyssey. New York: Modern Library, n.d.

KEITH, ARTHUR

A New Theory of Human Evolution. New York: Philosophical Library, 1949.

KEYNES, JOHN MAYNARD

The General Theory of Employment, Interest and Money. New York: Harcourt, Brace & Company, 1936.

LOCKE, JOHN

An Essay Concerning Human Understanding. London: George Routledge & Sons, Ltd., n.d.

MACHIAVELLI, NICCOLÒ

The Discourses. New York: Modern Library, n.d.

The Prince. New York: Modern Library, n.d.

MALTHUS, THOMAS

An Essay on Population. New York: E. P. Dutton & Co., 1933.

MARSHALL, ALFRED

Principles of Economics. London: Macmillan & Co., Ltd., 1930.

MARX, KARL

Capital. New York: Modern Library, n.d.

MONTESQUIEU, CHARLES LOUIS DE

De l'esprit des lois. Paris: Garnier, 1922.

MOSCA, GAETANO

The Ruling Class. New York: McGraw-Hill Book Company, 1939.

NIETZSCHE, FRIEDRICH

The Philosophy of Nietzsche. New York: Modern Library, n.d.

PARETO, VILFREDO

The Mind and Society. (4 vols.) New York: Harcourt, Brace & Company, 1935.

PLATO

The Republic. New York: Modern Library, n.d.

RICARDO, DAVID

Principles of Political Economy and Taxation. London: George Bell & Sons, Ltd., 1891.

ROBINSON, JOAN

The Economics of Imperfect Competition. London: Macmillan & Co., Ltd., 1933.

ROUSSEAU, JEAN JACQUES

The Social Contract and Discourses. New York: E. P. Dutton & Co., 1930.

SMITH, ADAM

An Inquiry into the Nature and Causes of the Wealth of Nations. New York: Modern Library, n.d.

SOMBART, WERNER

The Jews and Modern Capitalism. London: George Allen & Unwin, Ltd., 1913.

The Quintessence of Capitalism. New York: 1915.

SOROKIN, PITIRIM

Contemporary Sociological Theories. New York: Harper & Brothers, 1928.

SPENCER, HERBERT

The Principles of Sociology. New York: Appleton-Century-Crofts, Inc., 1908.

SPINOZA, BARUCH DE

The Philosophy of Spinoza. New York: Modern Library, n.d.

STEINDORFF, G., and SEELE, K. C.

When Egypt Ruled the East. Chicago: The University of Chicago Press, 1942.

TAWNEY, R. H.

The Acquisitive Society. New York: Harcourt, Brace & Company, 1920.

TOYNBEE, ARNOLD J.

A Study of History. (6 vols.) London: Oxford University Press, 1939.

TURGOT, A. R. J.

Reflections on the Formation and Distribution of Riches. London: Macmillan & Co., Ltd., 1898.

VEBLEN, THORSTEIN

The Theory of the Leisure Class. New York: Modern Library, n.d.

WALLAS, GRAHAM

The Great Society: A Psychological Analysis. New York: The Macmillan Company, 1923.

WEBER, MAX

Essays in Sociology. New York: Oxford University Press, 1946.

The Protestant Ethic and the Spirit of Capitalism. London: George Allen & Unwin, Ltd., 1930.

The Theory of Social and Economic Organization. London: William Hodge & Co., Ltd., 1947.

WILSON, J. A.

The Burden of Egypt. Chicago: The University of Chicago Press, 1951.

Index

Index